BACKCLOTH
TO
GAWTHORPE

MICHAEL P. CONROY

First Published 1971
Revised and enlarged 1996

ISBN 0 9528766 0 4

Computer type set in Times Roman

Published by M. P.Conroy 15, Hill Top Drive, Tottington. Bury. Lancs. BL8 3HN.

Printed by Lords of Burnley Ltd.

FRONTSPIECE

BARTON   **SHUTTLEWORTH**   **GRIMSHAW**

PARKER   **CATTERAL**

Colonel Richard Shuttleworth (Hugh's grand-son) Married Fleetwood Barton	Nicholas Shuttleworth Married Ellen Parker (Hugh's Parents)	Hugh Shuttleworth Held a coat of Arms with central Mullet in 1567 (Flower's Visitation of Lancashire)	Henry Shuttleworth of Hacking Married Catherine Catteral	Hugh Suttleworth Married Ann Grimshaw

WHITTAKER   **SHUTTLEWORTH**   **WORSLEY**

BARTON   **TALBOT**

Barnard Shuttleworth (Hugh's Brother) Married Jennetta Whitaker	Sir Richard Shuttleworth (Hugh's son) Married Margaret Barton	The Arms were without Mullet by 1605 (Note shield over front door)	Elizabeth Shuttleworth (Sister of Nicholas) Married Nicholas Talbot	Laurence Shuttleworth Married Elizabeth Worsley (Hugh's Grandparents)

Shields above the Main Entrance to the Long Gallery
(Shields drawn by Jock Shaw of the Lancashire Heraldry Group)

THE SHUTTLEWORTH COAT OF ARMS

HENRY DE SHUTTLEWORTH of Hapton was granted a Coat of Arms
in 1329

SHUTTLEWORTH of HAPTON
Argent, Three Weavers Shuttles Sable Tipped and Furnished Or with Quills
of Yarn, The Thread Dependant Or.

SHUTTLEWORTH of HACKING
Argent, between Three weavers Shuttles Sable Threaded Or, A Mullet Sable

4

CONTENTS

PEDIGREE OF THE GAWTHORPE SHUTTLEWORTHS

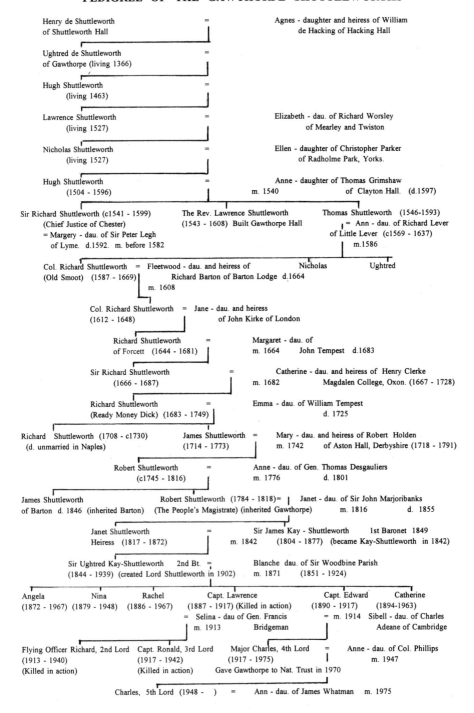

Henry de Shuttleworth = Agnes - daughter and heiress of William
of Shuttleworth Hall de Hacking of Hacking Hall

Ughtred de Shuttleworth =
of Gawthorpe (living 1366)

Hugh Shuttleworth =
(living 1463)

Lawrence Shuttleworth = Elizabeth - dau. of Richard Worsley
(living 1527) of Mearley and Twiston

Nicholas Shuttleworth = Ellen - daughter of Christopher Parker
(living 1527) of Radholme Park, Yorks.

Hugh Shuttleworth = Anne - daughter of Thomas Grimshaw
(1504 - 1596) m. 1540 of Clayton Hall. (d.1597)

Sir Richard Shuttleworth (c1541 - 1599)   The Rev. Lawrence Shuttleworth   Thomas Shuttleworth (1546-1593)
(Chief Justice of Chester)   (1543 - 1608) Built Gawthorpe Hall   = Ann - dau. of Richard Lever
= Margery - dau. of Sir Peter Legh   of Little Lever (c1569 - 1637)
of Lyme. d.1592. m. before 1582   m.1586

Col. Richard Shuttleworth = Fleetwood - dau. and heiress of   Nicholas   Ughtred
(Old Smoot) (1587 - 1669)   Richard Barton of Barton Lodge d.1664
m. 1608

Col. Richard Shuttleworth = Jane - dau. and heiress
(1612 - 1648) of John Kirke of London

Richard Shuttleworth = Margaret - dau. of
of Forcett (1644 - 1681) m. 1664 John Tempest d.1683

Sir Richard Shuttleworth = Catherine - dau. and heiress of Henry Clerke
(1666 - 1687) m. 1682 Magdalen College, Oxon. (1667 - 1728)

Richard Shuttleworth = Emma - dau. of William Tempest
(Ready Money Dick) (1683 - 1749) d. 1725

Richard Shuttleworth (1708 - c1730)   James Shuttleworth = Mary - dau. and heiress of Robert Holden
(d. unmarried in Naples)   (1714 - 1773) m. 1742 of Aston Hall, Derbyshire (1718 - 1791)

Robert Shuttleworth = Anne - dau. of Gen. Thomas Desgauliers
(c1745 - 1816) m. 1776 d. 1801

James Shuttleworth   Robert Shuttleworth (1784 - 1818)= Janet - dau. of Sir John Marjoribanks
of Barton d. 1846 (inherited Barton)   (The People's Magistrate) (inherited Gawthorpe) m. 1816 d. 1855

Janet Shuttleworth = Sir James Kay - Shuttleworth 1st Baronet 1849
Heiress (1817 - 1872) m. 1842 (1804 - 1877) (became Kay-Shuttleworth in 1842)

Sir Ughtred Kay-Shuttleworth 2nd Bt. = Blanche dau. of Sir Woodbine Parish
(1844 - 1939) (created Lord Shuttleworth in 1902) m. 1871 (1851 - 1924)

Angela   Nina   Rachel   Capt. Lawrence   Capt. Edward   Catherine
(1872 - 1967) (1879 - 1948) (1886 - 1967)   (1887 - 1917) (Killed in action)   (1890 - 1917) (1894-1963)
= Selina - dau of Gen. Francis   = m. 1914 Sibell - dau. of Charles
m. 1913 Bridgeman   Adeane of Cambridge

Flying Officer Richard, 2nd Lord   Capt. Ronald, 3rd Lord   Major Charles, 4th Lord = Anne - dau. of Col. Phillips
(1913 - 1940)   (1917 - 1942)   (1917 - 1975)   m. 1947
(Killed in action)   (Killed in action)   Gave Gawthorpe to Nat. Trust in 1970

Charles, 5th Lord (1948 -) = Ann - dau. of James Whatman m. 1975

ILLUSTRATIONS

Fig. 4 Gawthorpe Hall

FOREWORD

I think that the reader will agree that Mr. Conroy has given us a lively and instructive account of the life of my family at Gawthorpe.

It is a home that deserves to be recorded and I am grateful to him for his words and photographs.

My family kept very careful accounts, and those for the first half of the Seventeenth century have been published by the Chetham Society, and Mr. Conroy has been able to make skilful use of these. The family owned (and still owns) Barbon which is a property near Kirkby Lonsdale, and there is one entry about that which always seems to epitomise the difference between those days and these. Barbon provided the family with venison, and the entry runs "To a mane wch broughte a buke from Barbonne to Smytheles lls (two shillings); to a man wch. gyded him from Blackbourne 1111d."

Certainly it is a very happy thought that on £1000 of income my ancestors paid only £20 in tax; but some of this was collected by taxing windows which was really a tax on light and air and implies that the tax system was then (as now) in need of revision.

You will see a reference to Richard Shuttleworth who was knighted by King Charles II at Windsor. He married the daughter of the head of an Oxford College. She was known in Oxford at that time as "The Infanta' because it was a child-marriage - the combined ages of her and her husband being only 33. She was beautiful and an heiress, but her father compelled my ancestor to deposit £1000 in gold prior to the marriage.

By the Nineteenth century, life for the Shuttleworths had become much more comfortable. I enjoyed the account of their travelling by special train. It appeals to me as a favourable alternative to carrying my own bag. But that is progress! But life at Gawthorpe was certainly not luxurious. No great attention had been paid to escaping from the house in the event of a fire. The windows can be seen from the photographs to be small. Those that open are barred. I remember saying to Aunt Rachel "There's not much room is there?". "You can get through anything when there is a good fire behind you" she replied. I well remember the central heating in the 1940's. When it was on, it emitted nothing except a cold smell.

I was glad to read that McMaster looked after the children's pets so well. In my young days all rabbits were released as soon as our backs were turned at the end of the holidays. I generally spent these at Barbon, and in consequence the wild rabbits at Barbon developed a black and white look.

The reader will see a reference to the tradition of bibles being given to the school-children at St. Matthews. This still goes on to-day, and I intend to continue it until St. Matthews loses its identity, as I believe it is soon to be merged under a school reorganisation programme.

I should not like anyone reading this to suppose that my family was particularly grand or particularly important. The Shuttleworths were influential in this part of England for some 400 years, but they were only seldom national figures. What distinguished them is that they left behind them records of how they lived, and it is from these records that Mr. Conroy has given us this vivid account of their lives and times.

SHUTTLEWORTH

LECK HALL
1968

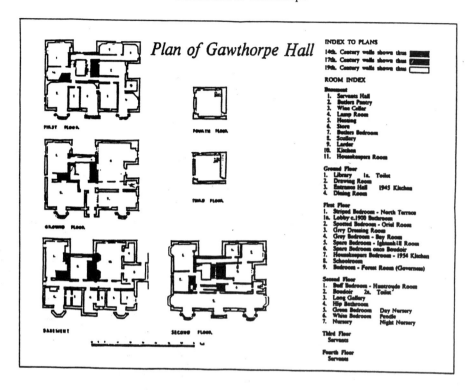

Plan of Gawthorpe Hall

FIRST FLOOR

GROUND FLOOR

BASEMENT

FOURTH FLOOR

THIRD FLOOR

SECOND FLOOR

INDEX TO PLANS
14th. Century walls shown thus
17th. Century walls shown thus
19th. Century walls shown thus

ROOM INDEX

Basement
1. Servants Hall
2. Butlers Pantry
3. Wine Cellar
4. Lamp Room
5. Heating
6. Store
7. Butlers Bedroom
8. Scullery
9. Larder
10. Kitchen
11. Housekeepers Room

Ground Floor
1. Library   1a. Toilet
2. Drawing Room
3. Entrance Hall   1945 Kitchen
4. Dining Room

First Floor
1. Striped Bedroom - North Terrace
1a. Lobby c.1900 Bathroom
2. Spotted Bedroom - Oriel Room
3. Grey Dressing Room
4. Grey Bedroom - Bay Room
5. Spare Bedroom - Ightenhill Room
6. Spare Bedroom once Boudoir
7. Housekeepers Bedroom - 1934 Kitchen
8. Schoolroom
9. Bedroom - Forest Room (Governess)

Second Floor
1. Buff Bedroom - Huntroyde Room
2. Boudoir   2a. Toilet
3. Long Gallery
4. Hip Bathroom
5. Green Bedroom   Day Nursery
6. White Bedroom   Pendle
7. Nursery   Night Nursery

Third Floor
Servants

Fourth Floor
Servants

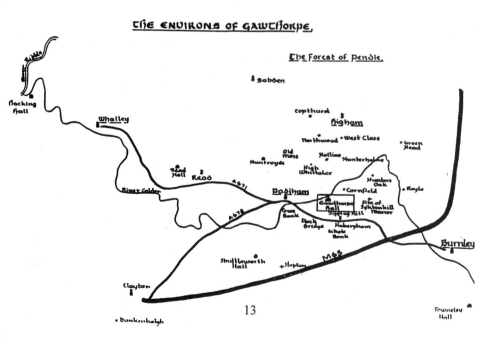

THE ENVIRONS OF GAWTHORPE.

The Forest of Pendle.

Ribble

Hocking Hall

Whalley

Read Hall

Read

River Calder

A671

A678

Sabden

Copthurst

Higham

Northwood   West Close

Old Moss

Huntroyde

Hollins

High Whittaker

Hunterholme

Green Head

Humbers Oak

Cornfield

Royle

Bodiham

Gawthorpe Hall

Site of Ightenhill Manor

Gross Bank

Ightenhill

Shuck Bridge

Haberginam Scholes Bank

Burnley

M65

Shuttleworth Hall

Ightton

Clayton

Dunkenhalgh

Towneley Hall

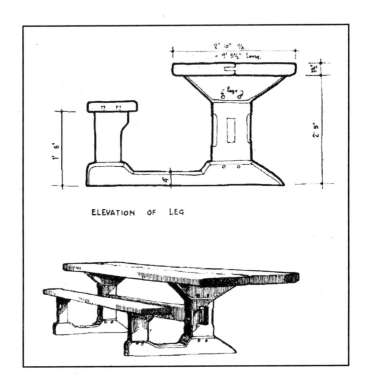

ELEVATION OF LEG

Table located in the basement when sketched in 1965

Miss Rachel said that this table dated back to c.1300

A shove Halfpenny board was marked out on one end of the table top

This table was in use up to the beginning of the Second World War

Fig. 7 The 14th Century Table

PREFACE

Many people have given valuable assistance in the preparation of this book and I acknowledge most gratefully my indebtedness to them.

Lord Charles Ughtred Shuttleworth M.C. kindly gave me permission to peruse the documents in the Gawthorpe. Estate Office and his aunt The Honourable Rachel Kay Shuttleworth allowed me access to her personal family pedigree and gave me permission to tape her invaluable reminiscences, as did her sister Mrs. Angela James. Mr. Roger Fulford also allowed me sight of his notes on the Shuttleworths and together with Lord Shuttleworth, his stepson, discussed the manuscript of this book at length with me before publication, which was most helpful.

I also wish to thank Mr. David Francis. C.Eng. A.M.I.C.E. who kindly drew all the illustrations; Mr. John Benson B.Sc. for his fine calligraphy work on the pedigree chart and environs plan and also Mrs. Elizabeth Benson for her elegant artistry in the production of the Coat of Arms in line drawing.

Professor C.T. Sandford M.A. (Econ) of Bath University of Technology gave me valuable advice and helpful criticism and Professor Angus McIntosh of Edinburgh University kindly translated the early fifteenth century parchment which was unearthed during my research in the old estate office at Gawthorpe.

P.B. Spurrier, Portcullis Pursuivant of Arms, helped with my queries regarding shields and Mr. John Kim ascertained the correct period of the dress in old family portraits. I also found the publications of my old tutor Mr. Bennett an excellent source of reference.

I am most grateful for the permission given by the Chetham Society to draw upon the invaluable information given in 'The House and Farm Accounts of The Shuttleworths', 1582 - 1621.

Finally I owe a deep debt of gratitude to Mrs. Pat Francis for transcribing the tape recordings into type and to Mrs. Gladys Craven and Miss Anne Conroy for the formidable task of typing the manuscript.

Fig. 5 The Hon. Rachel Shuttleworth grasping the Shuttle

Fig.6 The Old Tower

CHAPTER 1

THE ORIGINS OF GAWTHORPE

Any history of Gawthorpe, which is situated between Burnley and Padiham in North East Lancashire, is necessarily interwoven with the Shuttleworth family who have been connected with the estate since the 14th century. Gawthorpe and the Shuttleworths are also associated with weaving. The estate is situated in an old woollen weaving area which has become notable as a cotton weaving area. The derivation of the family name from a weaving shuttle, despite suggestions as to other origins, appears to be verified by one of the earliest documents in English discovered recently in the estate office. This gives the name as Schotilworth, 'Schotil' being an earlier spelling of 'Shuttle'. The embodiment of three shuttles in the family coat of arms and the later symbolism of the cubit arm in armour grasping a shuttle gives further evidence of this connection. The future role of Gawthorpe as a cultural centre for the practical study of textiles and craft, with its basis in the Kay Shuttleworth collection will consummate this long association. This connection with weaving may give us a clue as to the reason the Shuttleworths settled in that hamlet of Goukr (a Norse place name) between Padiham and the King's manor of Ightenhill, at this period.

We must first attempt to visualise the area at this time. It would consist of small hamlets carved out of the large deer forest next to the manor house of Ightenhill, where mares were kept to breed the horses for the King's Army. In the hamlet of Padiham, cotters had ceased to exist as a class by 1311, although in 1258 there had been 8 cotters, 25 villains, 9 or 10 tenants at will and one free tenant named Gilbert. There was a corn mill worth £2 per year and two free tenants, John of Whitaker (High Whittaker) and Richard son of Matthew. By 1332 seven men paid the subsidy, Richard of Whitaker, Richard of the Wood, William of Mikelbroke, Thomas son of Henry, Richard the Leadbeater, Adam of Antrim, and Henry son of John.

When in 1333, William of Gawthorpe, the hamlet next to Padiham, gave up nine and a half acres which he had cultivated, a new tenant could not be found until 1342 and then at a reduced rental of 2/2d per year. Who this new tenant was we do not know, but certainly the Shuttleworths were there in 1389 when land in the vill of Ightenhill was surrendered to the use of Ughtred de Shuttleworth by John del Eves. The Shuttleworth cadet had moved from his home at Shuttleworth Hall, Hapton, two miles away and we must surmise the reason. At Gawthorpe there was a tower four storeys high with walls about eight feet thick which had been either a watch tower, may be for the adjacent manor of the King at Ightenhill, or a Pele tower to watch, perhaps, for the marauding Scots (Fig.6). It had probably outlived its original purpose, and perhaps the "househunting" Shuttleworth found it an ideal situation for his pursuits. The nine and a half acres besides supplying corn would supply his sheep with pasturage and the ground floor of the tower would serve as a barn. His stores and wool could be kept on the first and second floors and the top floor, with its larger windows, would be ideal and safe for weaving. It was also convenient for the new fulling mill in Burnley, which was erected in 1296 opposite the parish church. The surrounding forest would supply both sport and meat for the relatively affluent gentleman, which we can assume that he was as a descendant of Henry de Shuttleworth and Agnes, daughter of William de Hacking of Hacking Hall. It may be coincidence that in 1394, John Shuttleworth, a Catholic priest, was installed in the chantry of Padiham St. Leonard's Church.

One of the earliest documents in English has been preserved in the estate office at Gawthorpe. It dates back to the early 15th century. (There are records of a John Parker at Ightenhill in 1440 and Ughtred Shuttleworth was living in 1389.)

THE EARLY 15TH CENTURY DOCUMENT IN ENGLISH

Fig. 8 The Early 15th Century Document

The document text reads :-

'Gracius & discret lord Parker of Hygtnill mutis I Huctrit of Schotilworth at ye kynkys suite in ye hall-mot of Hygtnill yt he covmn not wt his cornne yt grev at Gaucthopr yt he wonnis at to Brunlay milhen; and ye forsaid Huctrit gaf answar yt he forsaid plais aght not to cum to Brunlay milhen ne neuer dehed yis xl wyntir, for so lonke has it ban his, ne neuer herd tel be hold mon ne bi scriptur yt ye forsaid corhen aght to cum yedir. Yis lond is custum lond & ye corhen of it gos to ye kynkys milhen of Padiham & pais as other custumars don, wherfor it is no ler to ye kynke. Pryand yov yt I myght do so forth as ye forsaid plais has ban sesid all lordis and all stuard dais.

Ion Parker of Hygthnill sais he has fyned befor Roger Flovr sumtym chef stuard for a plais of lond yt hat Rohyll yt neuer was fyned for be-for tym, whege is gret los to ye kynke; pray and yov for ye kinkis avantage yt I myght haf a cope of ye record of his fyne & I sall gyf yov a bill of ye forsaid lond as layghe & custum will and y will say nomor when ye bedwn lefe.'

Which, translated into modern English means :-

'Gracious and discreet Lord, John Parker of Ightenhill accuses Ughtred of Shuttleworth at the King's suit in the hall-mote of Ightenhill that he did not come with his corn that grew at Gawthorpe where be lives to Burnley mill. And the aforesaid Ughtred gave answer that the aforesaid place was under no obligation to come to Burnley mill, and never did these last 4O years for it has been his that length of time, nor had he ever heard tell from old men, or in writings that the aforesaid corn should come thither. The land in question is custom-land and the corn from it goes to the King's mill of Padiham and he pays as other customers do, so the King incurs no loss from this. Praying you that I might continue to do as the aforesaid place has been seized in the time of all lords and all stewards.

John Parker of Ightenhill says he has paid a fee before Roger Flour, formerly chief steward, for a place of land that is called Royle, that has never been subject to such fee before, which is a great loss to the king; praying you for the advantage of the king that I might have a copy of the record of his fee; and I shall give you a deed of the aforesaid land as law and custom requires, and I will say no more, when you tell me to desist.'

The affluence of the Shuttleworths appears to have increased together with their social standing during the next 150 years. Of Ughtred's descendants, Laurence born about 1443, son of Hugh Shuttleworth, married Elizabeth Worsley, (one of the four daughters who were co-heirs of Richard Worsley of Downham, Twiston,) and their son Nicholas born about 1473 married Ellen daughter of Christopher Parker of Radholme Park, Co. York, and Bolland. In 1532 he covenanted with three Towneleys and others for the building of Burnley Church. Their son, Hugh, born in 1504, who died in 1596 aged 92, married Anne the daughter of Thomas Grimshaw of Clayton, and they had three sons, Richard born 1542, Laurence born 1545, and Thomas born about 1546. In 1500 the ancient deer grazing land had been granted out on fixed rent, and Shuttleworth had been granted parts of West Close and in the 1520's Shuttleworth had twenty five and a half acres in Ightenhill. Parts of the common fields had been enclosed in 1526, Stockbridge of 90 acres being amongst them. On 7th May 1526, Shuttleworth was among those classed as the 13 principal inhabitants of Habergham Eaves, which also included Habergham, Whitaker, Tattersall and Pickup (these, together with 80 others, were accused at the Duchy Court of entering a coal mine on Broadhead Moor and destroying it. According to Richard Towneley who owned it, Alexander Whatmaugh was running the mine unlawfully.)

In Padiham the woollen trade had been well established before 1600. The village had a church, reformed in 1573, Market Fair, shops and ale houses.

By 1588, the year of the Armada, the opulence of the Shuttleworths can be assessed by the fact that Mr. Hugh Shuttleworth was chosen as one of the gentlemen to lend money to the Crown. He lent £25, in that year and a further £50 in 1597.

Burnley, to the east of Ightenhill, expanded rapidly and by 1600 the Shuttleworths and the Towneleys were the two most influential families, 'The gentry' in fact.

Fig. 9 Sir Richard Shuttleworth

Fig. 10 Margaret, Sir Richard's wife

Fig. 11 Rev. Lawrence Shuttleworth

Fig. 12 The Long Gallery Fireplace

Fig. 13 The Old Tower incorporated in the Hall

Fig. 14 The Great Barn

23

CHAPTER 2

THE ELIZABETHAN HALL

Hugh's three sons, Richard, Laurence and Thomas, all played an important part in the rebuilding of the hall. Richard (Fig.9), the eldest, was born at Gawthorpe in 1541 but after his marriage lived at Smithills near Bolton which had been brought into the family by his wife (Fig.10), the widow of Robert Barton, Esq. Sir Richard was Chief Justice of Chester and was affluent enough to buy Barbon near Kirkby Lonsdale, Inskip on the Fylde and owned Forcett near Richmond in Yorkshire. When Hugh, Richard's father, died in 1596, Sir Richard probably decided to extend and renovate Gawthorpe. In 1597 Richard was included in the local group of "gentlemen of the best calling" along with Towneley, Starkie, Royle, Barcroft, Parker, Habergham, Nowell and Bannister. These were the gentlemen who were asked to lend money to the Crown, which was rarely repaid. Sir Richard loaned £50 in 1597. At this period Gawthorpe was situated on the edge of the great deer forests well stocked with red deer. The Calder running past Gawthorpe abounded in salmon and trout, the moors were full of grouse, there were partridges and hares, and otters were also hunted.

Sir Richard died in 1599 but his youngest brother had predeceased him in 1593. Thomas was steward to Sir Richard and had started and kept the famous Shuttleworth accounts from 1582 to his death. Richard's wealth and Thomas' precise accounting of it gave Laurence a firm foundation on which to carry out the rebuilding of Gawthorpe. As neither Richard nor Laurence had children it was Thomas's eldest son, Richard, later Colonel Richard, who succeeded to the estates. Thomas had married Anne, daughter of Richard Lever of Little Lever, in 1586 and had six children. One of his daughters, Ellen, married Sir Richard Assheton in Padiham.

The Rev. Laurence (Fig.11) succeeded in 1599 and stone was being quarried at the Delph at Gawthorpe for the extensions by the end of that year. This suggests that Sir Richard had laid the plans for the rebuilding before his death. Stone was also got from Schole Bank, and in Tinklers or Old Moss. Thus in the time of Elizabeth I the South facade and further additions to the West and East were added, making the hall foursquare and with an E of three bays on the South to commemorate the period of the "Great Queen"; the Shuttleworth arms (argent, three shuttles sable tipped and threaded or) were placed in the centre over the front door. The first stone was laid on 26th August 1600.

The hall of Gawthorpe was "reared" up to the roof in June 1602, each floor being marked externally by a string course (Fig.13), and the workmen were entertained by a piper to celebrate rearing day. In this year, too, the common cultivated land that remained was enclosed. Laurence Shuttleworth, as the largest copyholder and freeholder in Padiham was granted approximately 120 acres in the East of Padiham, 140 acres at High Whittaker, 10 acres at Copthurst and 40 acres at Schole Bank.

The Great Barn (Fig.14) was being erected at the same time; in 1604 the accounts state that 609 yards of slate @ 4d cost £10. 3. 0. In these days travelling was arduous; in 1605, when 3 men went from Gawthorpe to York and back they used 8 horses and the charges for victuals were 9/-d for horsemeat and 9/3d for the men.

The screen in the Great Hall at Gawthorpe was begun in 1605 and on shields on the East side can be seen the initials of Hugh and Richard and on the West side of Laurence and Thomas. Underneath each is the initial of the person's station in life, G for Gentleman; P for Presbyter; and K for Knight.

H, S.	1605	R. S.		L. S.	1605	T. S.
G.		K.		P.		G.

At this time there appear to have been 10 male servants including steward, bailiff, farming men and a carter, whose aggregate wages were £15. 13. 4 per annum. There, were 4 female servants including a housekeeper, the aggregate of whose annual wages were only £3. 10. 0. Out of this total of £19. 3. 4 for 14 people, Edward Sherburne the steward received £3. 6. 8 per annum in 1603.

Wool was still being produced at Gawthorpe during this period. In 1605 there is an entry in the accounts for £8. 15. 0 received for "last year's wool" and in 1606 it was £9. 9. 0.

CHAPTER 3

THE INFLUENCE OF GAWTHORPE ON PADIHAM

The influence of Gawthorpe was particularly felt in Padiham. In 1605 the Shuttleworth lands consisted of 29½ oxgangs and 5 acres together with 22 tofts. The oxgangs were all galded at 10/-d an oxgang towards the building of the schoolhouse and smithy at the West end of Padiham, and consisted of 20 at High Whitaker, 2 late Listers land, 2 late Haydocks, 2 late Willasells, 1½ late Bannisters, 1 late Cockshots, ½ late Robinsons and ½ at Copthurst. The 5 acres were at Dubcar, late Marshalls oxgang. A note was made by Laurence Shuttleworth of the tofts in Padiham that belonged to him - a toft being an enclosure generally on the side of a homestead, or a field where a building or a house once stood. It could also be a grove of trees. His tofts included Bondyard, Whipcroft, Bridgend, the Chamber of the Hill, the Acre of the Chapel, the Priest's Chamber, Black Hall and the Bank House.

High Whitaker is a farm on the banks of High Whitaker Clough immediately on the North bank of the River Calder and to the North of Gawthorpe. On this site was Whitaker Old Hall, the seat of a branch of the Whitakers from 1333 or earlier. Amongst the traditions is one to the effect that in the Old Hall of Whitaker was a skilfully devised priest's hole. It is not certain when the estate came into the hands of the Shuttleworths but it had consisted of 100 acres of arable land, 100 of pasture, 20 of meadow, 100 of moor and morass in High Whitaker, Simonstone and Padiham and was in the possession of the Shuttleworths in 1582. Simonstone in this period mainly belonged to the Shuttleworths and in 1617 half a year's rent was 13/4d. Tipping Hill in Padiham had the same rent and also belonged to Gawthorpe. Westclose was also part of the estate lying to the South of the village of Higham. In 1598 Sir Richard Shuttleworth paid the quarters rent, tythe corn rent and a relief for West Close. (A relief being the sum of money which the new tenant paid to the landlord on the death of his ancestor.) One of the family appears to have lived at Copthurst, another at Cornfield. Crocklewood was also in the possession of the family. The Schole Bank estates were sold to Gawthorpe in 1586 by Ingram Wyllasell for a certain sum in hand and an annuity.

The Shuttleworths also owned the lease of the Mill in Padiham and meal was sold there in 1611 at 4/8d the mett. (A mett is a measure, usually one bushel). Fairs were held twice yearly on May 8th and September 26th, mainly for coopers and other wooden ware. There was in this period a lengthy lawsuit with Burnley regarding fairs. Padiham complained that Burnley's fairs infringed, Burnley said that Padiham had no right to hold fairs.

Various local shops dealt with Gawthorpe. In 1611 John Starkie, the chandler, sold 13½ yards of taffeta to the mistress of Gawthorpe for 6/-d. He also sold candles, currants, whalebone, white jean fustian, cambrics end woodcocks amongst his many wares. Richard Hanson's wife sold ale and "aquavita", while Widow Sankey sold bread, wheatcakes, powdered sugar, ale and claret. Shoes, sweet-soap, loaves of sugar and buttons could be purchased locally. At this time soap cost 9d a ball, a lb. of household soap cost 4d and "sweet" soap with which to wash oneself cost between 4½d and 6d a lb. Sparrows cost 1d a dozen, snipes a 1d each and varnish (for beds) 1/4d a lb. Butter cost 3/-d a stone in Padiham market.

The piper of Padiham came round to Gawthorpe and on one visit in 1609 was given 1/-d. This was not the first time pipers had visited Gawthorpe. When the Hall was reared to the roof the pipes were played for the various local craftsmen who were involved in the building. Timber for Gawthorpe had come from Read and Mitton although some came from Ireland; there is an entry of 956 pieces via Hoole in 1607. (387 rafter timbers and 569 panel boards also came in August of that year) In May 1606 a wright was paid 6d a day for working 6 days at the planks for the stable, and also for felling trees in Read Wood. A cooper in Padiham received 6d for girding two brewery vessels several times and in 1602, 6d for a day and a half's work mending vessels in the house. Two men working at Ryecliffe for the stone for Gawthorpe had 6d a day and provided their own meals in September, 1600. In that month as much stone was hewn there and at Schole bank as costs £5. 13. 4 - free stone costing 2½d per yard and wall stone 2d. Stone from Padiham Moor cost more, it was 3d per yard. Scholebank the farm is situated on the banks of the stream which falls from Rosegrove to Padiham - Schoolbank is noted as early as 1591 as also Schoolhouse Hagge, or enclosure, showing that at that early period a school existed in the neighbourhood.

As owners of this land, the Shuttleworths had their responsibilities. They had to pay a local tax or gald towards the pinder or keeper of the common pound or pinfold in Padiham. They also had to pay towards the upkeep of the local constable. In 1612 for example they had to pay 3/10d to the constable for taking the Padiham witch, Margaret Pearson, to Lancaster (she was later pilloried in Padiham and also in Whalley, Clitheroe and Lancaster for her supposed witchcraft). In 1620, Shuttleworths also paid half a fifteenth to the Constable of Padiham for 'the watching of the supposed witches'. It has already been noted that a day's wage for a cooper was 4d and a stonemason 6d. At this time coal from the local pit was 4d a quarter, while in 1613 clerks from the churches of Burnley and Padiham received 7d in wages and by 1618 this was 8d.

The church in Padiham had been reformed about 1574 and in 1607 there was a nave of 17 forms. In the first form the bench rent was 1/6d in the first 'quire' and 'pue' and this was decreased by 1d for each form back. In 'quires' sat the Rileys, Shuttleworths, Haberghams, Ashtons, Starkies and Andertons. Out of a seating for 210 only 161 were let.

By 1838 the Shuttleworths held most of the Tithe Lands at the east end of Padiham, the Starkies lands being mainly on the west side.

CHAPTER 4

LOCAL CONNECTIONS WITH THE SHUTTLEWORTHS
IN THE SEVENTEENTH CENTURY

By the end of the 16th century the Shuttleworths had many connections with people in Burnley and the surrounding district. Burnley was a hamlet in which the Shuttleworths held the watermill and leased it to Mr. John Towneley of Hurstwood at the yearly rent of £26.13.4 paid in two halves, one on St.Matthias' Day, 24th February, and also on St. Michael's Day, 29th September. The stewards or bailiffs at Gawthorpe, such as Abraham Coulthurst, who was there in 1594 and whose daughter married Henry Towneley, attended the Burnley fairs held on 6th March, Easter Eve, 6th and 13th May, 10th July and 11th October, chiefly to buy and sell cattle. Horses and sheep were also for sale. Thomas Yate was a bailiff to Sir Richard Shuttleworth and in 1599 his year's wages were 40/-d. Later he became steward to Colonel Richard Shuttleworth, Sir Richard's nephew. An Anthony Wilkinson was also steward for Colonel Richard in 1608/9. The steward was a very responsible person and received a higher emolument, in 1603 for instance, steward Edward Sherburne, received £3.6.8., as his annual wage. The Shuttleworths had to pay towards the 3/15ths in Habergham (a 1/15th was the fifteenth part of moveable goods) and in January 1617 it was 1/10½d towards the original grant of Burnley Market. A heifer in calf cost about £2.15.0 in 1601 and a fat calf 6/-d. If any of the cattle had to be killed at Gawthorpe a butcher would come and do it. In 1619 the charge was 4d - the same price for a man 'watching and warding' in Burnley Fair in 1620.

The Shuttleworths also took their cattle to sell at Preston Guilds and fairs. Preston Guilds were held in 1582, 1602 and 1622, at twenty year intervals; hence the local saying 'once every Preston Guild' meaning 'once in a long time'.

On one of his visits to Chester in 1595 Sir Richard took Robert Nutter from Greenhead. As they returned through Cheshire, Robert complained to Richard that he had been bewitched by Chattox (one of the Pendle witches) just as his father Christopher Nutter had been bewitched by Chattox's daughter Anne Redfearn in 1593, two years previously. Robert died in Cheshire and in 1612 Chattox was executed at Lancaster Castle for his murder, and Anne

Redfearn, her daughter was executed for the murder of his father Christopher. As the Chattox's lived on Shuttleworth lands, at West Close, the Shuttleworths had to pay 6d as landowners for the transporting of Bess Chattox' clothes to Lancaster in 1613. Bess was Chattox other daughter but she was not convicted of witchcraft.

The Shuttleworths of Hacking were close relatives of Sir Richard. Next to Sir Richards name over the fireplace in the drawing room at Gawthorpe is the name of his uncle Richard Shuttleworth of Hacking Hall, and Richard's wife Anne. Uncle Richard was the brother of Hugh and was the last of the Shuttleworths of Hacking because, having no son, his daughter Anne was heiress, according to Bishop Shuttleworth's pedigree. She married Sir Thomas Walmsley and the panel on the extreme left of the fireplace depicts this. Sir Thomas was said to have acquired his wealth by great rapacity at law and his marriage to a rich heiress. The heiress was Anne Shuttleworth of Hacking. Judge Walmsley rebuilt Hacking Hall and acquired Dunkenhalgh. In 1713 there was to be another heiress, this time Catherine Walmsley who married Lord Petre. He died of smallpox at fourteen years of age, she was then fifteen and with child. The child became the eighth Lord Petre.

The Shuttleworths, Parkers, Towneleys and Starkies were all influential in the area at this time and as the gentry of the area, associated with each other. There was a Parker at Extwistle in 1602 who bought three in-calf heifers from Gawthorpe for £8. 3. 4d and venison was sent to Gawthorpe from Mr. Parker of Browsholme in 1610 and the man who brought it had 2/6d as his fee.

John Starkie and Col. Richard examined an Edmund Robinson of Pendle Forest (whose father was a mason) in connection with some of the Lancashire witches in 1633. It was on this evidence that a number of women were apprehended. (John Starkie was the son of Nicholas and grandson of Edmund whose father was Laurence Starkie) Edmund had repaid £8. 6. 8 to Col. Richard in 1611 at 21½% interest!. John is not to be confused with a John Starkie who is mentioned in the accounts as being a chandler in Padiham.

The Shuttleworths also had connections with the Paslews of Wiswell, the family that gave the Monastery of Whalley its last abbott. It is noted that Francis Paslew sent a letter to Gawthorpe in 1613 and the woman who brought it was given 4d. Mr. Sergeant Walmsley (later Sir Thomas) had even closer connections and in 1587, £50 was received from him. His initials can be seen over the fireplace in the drawing room at Gawthorpe, as was stated earlier.

Colonel Richard and his brothers, Nicholas and Ughtred, went to Burnley Grammar School and in 1598 John Woodruffe was paid £8. 12. 6 for their board, while 'Birchall's wife' appears to have been the local washerwoman and in April 1610 received 8d for a quarter's washing for the youths, Henry Shuttleworth and Laurence Shuttleworth.

Other locals at this time were Mary Ainsworth who brought strawberries to Gawthorpe in 1612 and received 3d, Thomas Parker and Roger Wood who were engaged in veterinary practice in the area and Thomas Yate, another faithful servant of the Shuttleworth family, to whom there is a brass plate in Padiham Church. He seems to have made periodic journeys to London when sums of money were entrusted to him to make purchases and payments. He also went to Manchester, Wigan, York, Stourbridge fairs etc. and received an annual wage of £3. 6. 8. in the years 1613 - 1617 -- the same rate as James Yate when he was promoted steward. Whilst in London Thomas probably met a namesake of his, Mr. Yate of Greys Inn Lane who was the host of the Shuttleworths in London until they bought their house in Islington. In December 1609 he received 30/-d for 'diet'.

There also appears to have been a James Yate who was a glazier in Burnley in 1596 for he is noted as putting 3 windows in Burnley Grammar School. In 1619 the Parish Church clock went wrong and John Singleton was called upon to mend it. The churchwarden, Nicholas Halstead, was paid 2/6d for the food for this man during this time.

The Shuttleworths had to pay galds to the Constables of the chapelries or townships of Burnley, Padiham and Habergham Eaves and also to the grave or bailiff of the Forest of Pendle. The amount of a 15th was payable by the Shuttleworths in respect of their property, assessed as so much on every oxgang of land. In Padiham it was 3/10d and in Burnley 7½d in the first decade of the 17th century. They also paid to the ducking stool and whipping post at Burnley which was half a fifteenth in 1611 -- 15 pence.

During the period 1605-1620 waits and fiddlers came to Gawthorpe from Halifax, individual players and groups such as Disley and his Company of players, Thomas Yates and Two Fiddlers, Dynley and piper, Alex Grundy and piper, Arthur Gurney the piper, and the piper of Padiham. Other sets of players also toured the area and had performed at Smithills. Such players as Lord

Morleys, Sir Peter Lyghes, Earl of Derbys, Lord Monteagles, Lord Stafford and the Queen's Players besides groups from Rochdale, Garstang, Blackburn and Downham.

Over the latter part of his life Laurence was disturbed by a claim from the Crown extending over the greater part of the Gawthorpe estate. He died in February 1608 at his Warwickshire Rectory. Probably his-sister-in-law (the widow of Thomas) had continued to reside at Gawthorpe with her children and the eldest child, Richard, Laurence's nephew succeeded at the age of 21.

Fig. 15 Colonel Richard Shuttleworth

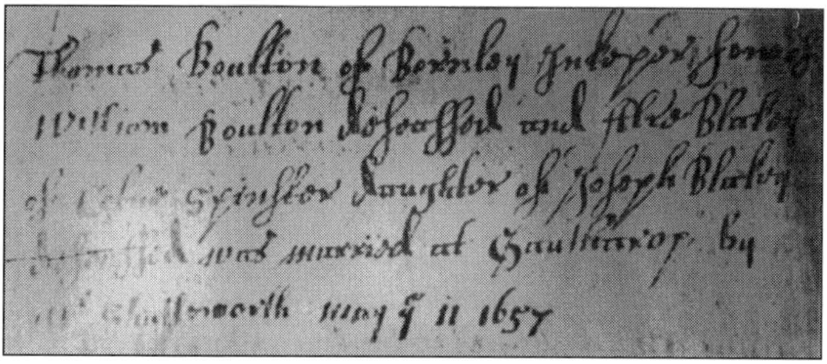

Fig. 16 Extract from Burnley Parish Church Register 1657

Backcloth to Gawthorpe

Fig. 17 Fleetwood Barton,
Richard's wife

Fig. 18 Richard & Fleetwood's Bed

CHAPTER 5

THE ERA OF COLONEL RICHARD SHUTTLEWORTH

Richard (Fig.15) married Fleetwood Barton (Fig.18), the heiress of Barton in Amoulderness who brought that estate into the Shuttleworth family.

In the year that he succeeded to Gawthorpe Richard and his wife travelled to London on horseback, returning by carouche. His dress was a high crowned hat adorned with lace and a band of coloured silk with an edging of green silk. A wide ruff around his neck, doublet (long waistcoat) lined with linen and decorated with embroidery and coloured buttons, jerkin (jacket) of coloured friese with slashed sleeves and ornamented with buttons and lace, large padded breeches to the knee, silk hose, buckled shoes, heavily embroidered cloak and velvet girdle, dagger and sword. Mistress Shuttleworth wore a richly trimmed hat, ruff and collar (Fig.17), bodice covering stiff stays of leather, a hooped skirt held away from the body by wires, whalebone or leather, fashionable shoes and a bright cloak of branched satin adorned with fine orange coloured wool and paris buttons.

The children of the Shuttleworths sometimes dressed in the same fashion as their elders but the apprentice boys on the farm had sheepskin doublets lined with canvas. Their best wear was doublet of fustian lined with linen, blue cloth breeches and a long cloak with fancy buttons.

Richard spent his time supervising his farm and lands at Padiham, Filly Close, West Close and Ightenhill. He sold horses, sheep, lambs, oxen, ducks and poultry as well as wheat. He also attended to Church and parish affairs and went to markets and fairs besides visiting and entertaining friends. At Christmas there were feasts and wassailing and in 1609 maids coming with the wassail bowl were given 12d.

As a wealthy man Richard had many local demands made upon him, there were many levies of repair of highways and bridges, for maimed soldiers, for military expeditions, for maintenance of paupers and repair of churches at Burnley and Whalley.

Although he lent £30 to King James in 1612 Colonel Richard found himself involved in lawsuits with the King about his copyholds in Pendle Forest which the king claimed were essay lands. He had to pay James a considerable sum of money for this and, as the monarch was short of money he leased to Richard the two cornmills of Burnley and Padiham, Burnley for 66/8d which he sub-leased to Towneley for £26.13.4 per year. These incidentally were the two mills mentioned in the Ughtred Shuttleworth Document of the 1420's.

The goods bought by the household during this period indicate the kind of life they led. These include playing cards, pipe and tobacco, fiddles, lute, suits of armour, muskets, pistols, gauntlets and swords. Delicacies included almonds, aniseed, macaroons, Naples biscuits, raisins, cloves, dates, sugar and pepper, plums, damsons, cherries, apples and oranges. Besides mutton, beef, chicken, and fish, they ate venison and larks, plovers, sparrows and pigeons and drank milk and small and strong beer.

As a pastime hawking was popular at Gawthorpe as is shown by the entries in the accounts of hawks, hoods, bells, and daggs.

Various items of clothing were bought for the servants, included in these were, in 1611, 7½ yards of canvas cloth for shirts for John Leigh costing 5/11d, 5½ yards of cloth for two shirts for Abel cost 5/0½d and in 1613 5 yards of cloth for two shirts for Hargreaves cost 4/8d. The latter also received stockings costing 11d in 1612, stockings for Roger Isherwood costing 2/0d in 1610 and for Mr, Barton 3/0d in 1613. By comparison, for weaving woollen cloth in 1611 the weaver received 1d per yard. Linen cloth in 1605 wove at 2d per yard and canvas from hemp at 1¼d per yard. In 1620 napkins wove at 1½d a yard. There are also items which state that in 1611 2 lbs of wool brought to weave into cloth for Lee and Leigh's clothes cost 12d, while dressed wool and fustians cost roughly double this in 1618.

In 1617 2/0d a stone was paid to John Roe for spinning wool for blankets. The weaving cost half this amount as did the dighting and frizing which was paid to James Hill. The spinning, weaving, dighting and frizing of coarser wool for the blankets of the servants cost 4/0d for 7 yards, whilst James Pollard dressed, spun, dyed and wove 14 yards of red cloth for 25/0d (for gentlemen's coats it cost 2/7½d a yard).

This was the period of the Lancashire witches and in 1620 half a fifteenth was paid to the constable of Padiham for watching the supposed witches. This was the quota of Richard Shuttleworth to the levy of 2½d for Padiham.

Richard had become Sheriff of Lancashire in 1617, (this was the year that James I came to Hoghton Tower - Barton Manor having a mysterious fire at this time). He was again Sheriff in 1637 and a J.P. The Sheriff was appointed for one year and exercised general control over the County. When taxes were levied the Sheriff decided what amount each hundred should pay. He was assisted by bailiffs.

John Starkie was also a J.P. and in 1636 he sent three Padiham men to Whalley Assizes for non-observance of Lent and other days. These Puritans were Barnard Halliday, Henry Denby and butcher Thomas Cockshott. They were fined 5/0d each. (It is interesting to note that in 1685 the Denbys were again in trouble, John Denby of Padiham, Cordwainer, was sent by John Starkie to Preston Jail for uttering treasonable words while in the custody of John Shuttleworth, Constable of Padiham).

In 1641, being the M.P. for Preston in the Long Parliament and during the Commonwealth, Richard Shuttleworth was enjoined by the House of Commons to see the ordinance of the militia enforced in Lancashire. In 1642 hostilities broke out in the Civil War and Richard was made a Colonel of the Parliamentary Army when he commanded the hundred of Blackburn.

On October 17th, 1642, Parker, Habergham, Halstead, Barcroft, Ingham and others from Pendle, Colne and Clitheroe were invited to attend Gawthorpe on the following Thursday to adopt definite plans for action in the Parliamentary cause. The meeting was badly attended but orders were sent out by Shuttleworth and Starkie that all men between sixteen and sixty should muster at Padiham at ten o'clock on 24th October, with arms, powder and shot. Four of Col. Richard's sons, Ughtred, Edward, William and Nicholas were made captains. Captain William has slain at Lancaster in March 1643. Colonel Richard's eldest son, Richard, also a Colonel, died in 1648 (Fig.19).

On April 20th, 1643 the Earl of Derby attempted to capture Gawthorpe but his troops were waylaid by the Roundheads at Read. On June 15th Col. Richard was wounded at Colne and routed by Sir Charles Lucas and in 1648 hostilities again broke out and the Lancashire militia was put under Nicholas Shuttleworth who was promoted to Colonel. Charles I was executed on January 30th, 1649 and then began the disbandment of the County levies, which was not easily accomplished. The forces under Col. Shuttleworth complained about their pay which was long overdue. The forces at Lancaster marched to Clitheroe and fortified themselves there. Eventually the soldiers agreed to withdraw and Clitheroe Castle was dismantled and demolished by order of Parliament, who voted the sum of £1200 to the forces of the County under the command of Col. Nicholas.

In 1646 Col. Richard was appointed one of the laymen of the 3rd Lancashire Presbyterian classis and in 1650, the Ecclesiastic Commissioner and active magistrate for the County. He was Sequestrator of estates of the 'delinquents' in Lancashire and the Burnley Parish Church registers show that he was one of the judges appointed for solemnisation of marriages (Fig.16). He had been allocated the Stansfield Chapel in St. Peter's Church in 1634, where he had the front pew. As he was a Presbyterian, his officiating at Church ceremonies does not seem to have been appreciated by Burnley people as a whole.

By 1610 Padiham had 232 families, 1106 souls, but from 1650 to 1816 the Shuttleworths were living mainly at Forcett, near Richmond. It was in 1650 that Col. Richard was formally dismissed from employment in connection with the Lancashire militia when it was re-organised, being out of sympathy with the existing Government. He did, however, meet Colonel Lilliburn at Hoghton Tower in 1651 although estranged from Cromwell.

In 1660 Colonel Richard's income from his lands in the hundred of Blackburn was £1000 of which he paid £20 tax. He was also mining coal under this land as early as 1640.

The first edition of Whitakers 'Whalley' stated that Colonel Richard was 'a Wary, fawning man who knew how to serve the time, in the worst sense of the words, and fattened, along with his brother sequestrators, upon the spoils of better houses than his own. In the dialect of the neighbourhood he is yet remembered as Old Smoot ('Smooting along' means one who travels in a wily fashion) a term which conveys no bad idea of the demure and plausible hypocrite of those times...'

It appears that 'Old Smoot' had made himself so unpopular in Lancashire that, on his death, his descendants continued to live at Forcett in Gilling, Yorkshire.

Fig. 19 Colonel Richard Shuttleworth Junior

Fig. 20 Richard of Forcett

CHAPTER 6

LEGACIES OF THE SEVENTEENTH CENTURY

By 1660 householders were being taxed at 2/0d for each £5 on incomes of £5 and over. Burnley contributed £84. 13. 6 which was paid by 34 householders, 205 married men each paying 6d and 190 unmarried persons who paid 1/6d each. Richard Shuttleworth paid £20, Richard Towneley £10, Nicholas Towneley £10, John Habergham £10, Elizabeth Towneley £6, George Halstead £2. 8. 0 and John Ingham £1. 14. 0.

In his Will made on June 11th 1668, Col. Richard Shuttleworth then aged 81 left:-

£5 to his clerk and late servant Lawrence Osbaldeston.

£5 to his servant and solicitor Jno. Crooke if he dwelt with him at the time of his death.

£2. 10. 0 to servant Richard Radcliffe.

All his plate to his son Barton Shuttleworth and £1 to Mr. Clayton of Blackburn to preach at his funeral.

All his remaining personal property was to be divided into two parts, one to his four natural sons, Nicholas, Barton, John and Edward and his three natural daughters, Anne, Margaret and Ellinor but for a fifth part to go to grandson Nicholas and granddaughter Fleetwood, children of his late son Richard. His servant Roger Barton and his son Barton were to be his sole executors.

Thus when he died in June 1669, aged 82, the eldest grandson Richard (Fig.20), who was born in 1644, succeeded to the estates, which included Gawthorpe, Forcett, Barton and Barbon. This was the son of Richard Shuttleworth M.P. for Clitheroe who had also been a Colonel in the Parliamentary Army and had died in 1648 (Fig.19).

When Richard Shuttleworth of Forcett died in 1680 his Will stated that he wished to be buried in the Church of Forcett. He left his estates to his son Richard (later Sir Richard Shuttleworth) (Fig.21) and

£100 to Richard son of his brother Nicholas

£200 to Thomas son of his brother Nicholas

£300 to Elizabeth daughter of his brother Nicholas

£200 to Fleetwood daughter of his brother Nicholas

£200 to Nicholas son of his brother Nicholas out of Richard's
    lands in Yorkshire, Lancashire and Westmoreland.

£200 to his sister Heath Tempest (her husband Rowland receiving £30)

£30 annuity to his sister Fleetwood Lambton

£20 annuity to his cousin Barbara Lambton

£10 to William Sudell and wife to buy mourning

To pay these legacies he ordered the timber in his parks at Barbon to be cut down.

£50 went to his brother Nicholas

£10 per annum for the poor of Forcett forever or £160 in lieu.

All his plate, jewels and rings went to his wife Margaret and his son Richard. His wife also had his dwellinghouse at Forcett and £20 annuity for life. This son Richard was knighted by Charles II at Windsor in 1684, so that it would appear that the Shuttleworths were prepared to accept the Stuarts and their policy at this period.

These Wills serve to show the extent of the Shuttleworth's fortunes at this time. Around Gawthorpe the Shuttleworths possessed the lands and farms at High Whittaker, Copthurst and Filly Close. In Burnley they held 33 acres of land and farms near the Municipal hospital, nearly 70 acres at Broadhead, mostly near the Summit, the lease of Ightenhill Park and Burnley Corn Mill. (The oldest corn mill in Burnley was the Kings Mill in Bridge Street, originally leased from the Crown by the Shuttleworths at a rent of £3. 6. 8. The Shuttleworths sub-let to tenants. In the 18th Century the tenants were John Taylor, John Halstead, William Crook and Henry Crook, all relations by marriage.)

Fig. 21 Sir Richard Shuttleworth the Second

Fig. 22 'Ready Money Dick' Shuttleworth

CHAPTER 7

THE SHUTTLEWORTHS IN THE EIGHTEENTH CENTURY

The second Sir Richard Shuttleworth (Fig.21) succeeded to Gawthorpe in 1680 at fourteen years of age, went to Oxford when he was sixteen, married Catherine (aged fifteen) the daughter of Doctor Clerke, Head of Magdalen College the same year, had an heir Richard (later 'Ready Money Dick') when he was seventeen, was knighted when eighteen (probably a device for inheriting the estates before coming of age) and died, after fathering two more children, at twentyone! He was buried in front of the altar rails in Padiham Church. As his father-in-law had also died at Gawthorpe earlier, it is no wonder that Catherine, aged twenty and with three children, stayed away from Lancashire and lived at Forcett. This probably became the family home for over a hundred years and it was not until 1818 that the next Shuttleworth was to be buried in Padiham. Gawthorpe was still the Family Seat.

The heir of Sir Richard, also a Richard (Ready Money Dick)Shuttleworth (Fig.22), and his heir, James (Fig.24) were both M.P.'s. Richard was Tory M.P. for Lancashire during the ten Parliaments 1705-49 and Father of the House.

In 1716 a number of freeholders and copyholders of Burnley drew up a document allowing Richard Shuttleworth to take more water from the River Brun near the Parish Church by constructing a wall or weir to divert the water into a watercourse and so to the corn mill (Fig.23). The document translated into modern English makes interesting reading :-

BURNLEY MILL WATER WITH SEVERAL HANDS FOR IT

We whose names are subscribed freeholders and copyholders within and of the manor of Ightenhill of intent that the mill of Richard Shuttleworth Esq., in Burnley called Burnley mill may be better supplied with water got for the common good of the inhabitants of the town and township of Burnley and Habergham Eaves for our selves severally and for our several and respective heirs servants and agents with and do hereby give full and free liberty license power and authority to the said Richard Shuttleworth and his heirs his and their agents servants and undertakers and shall henceforth at all or any time or times hereafter at his or their own will and pleasure dig trench drive and sough one mill stream, mill race or water course for his said mill at Burnley aforesaid in and through the waste ground within Burnley aforesaid hereafter mentioned (that is

Fig. 23 1716 Water Mill Document

Fig. 24 James Shuttleworth and Family

to say) in and through a certain portion of ground called Burnley Royds to a place called Bank floodgate through which race or watercourse to bring and convey water out of the River or Brook in Burnley aforesaid called Brown forward also Burnley water to the mill aforementioned and shall and may likewise fix rest and attach a wall or weir transverse the said River or Brook for the better turning and driving the water into the said mill race or watercourse without the least disturbance or interruption of us or our heirs and may likewise from time to time and at all times hereafter as there shall be occasion enforces and keep open the said watercourse and keep the same in good order and repair the banks to convey and carry the water to the said mill.

WITNESS where so of we have hereto set our hands and seals the sixth of December, A.D. 1716.

John Townley	R. Kippax	Rich Towneley
Tho Whitaker	E. Townley	Tho Towneley
	Henry Halstead Jr	G. Parker
	Robt Whitaker	Jno Hadock
	Geo Hargreaves	Jno Jackson
	John Eastwood	John Jackson
	J. Holden	John Sager
	James Whitaker	

James Shuttleworth was Tory M.P. for Preston 1741-54 (where he had a town house in Winkley Square) and for Lancashire 1761-8. James and his father were so critical of the Whigs that they were regarded as Jacobites and it may be that Francis Towneley visited Gawthorpe in 1745 to gather troops for the Jacobite Rebellion. It may well be that the hoard of coins found under the window ledge of the small room in the East Wing which was removed during the Barry renovations of 1850 was left by the Jacobite, Francis Towneley.

During the period that the family resided at Forcett, Gawthorpe fell into disrepair and even the drawing-room was used as a granary at this time. James' son, Robert Shuttleworth, the great grandson of Sir Richard, rectified this, replacing the oak panelled stair case and commenced refitting and refurnishing the house. It was about this period that the River Calder was diverted to the other side of the valley because of pollution. Family tradition has it that Robert had eloped with Anne Deseguliers. James, his father, had pursued them but was captivated by a dainty foot as she was stepping into a carriage. On learning that it was the new Mrs. Shuttleworth he was reconciled with his son!

The estate had a restrictive influence on the development of Padiham, where its position influenced the shape and industries of the town. Until the 1840's the landowners prevented the building of factories and Padiham was a village of handloom weavers cottages, while Burnley's power loom factories were developing rapidly. Yet 700-800 weavers from Clayton and Padiham joined Burnley weavers at a meeting at Gannow Top on November 15th 1819 and there were riots against the higher wages for spinners. In 1830 the Padiham Chartists prided themselves on their banner inscribed "sell thy garment and buy a sword". The average weekly wage per head of the population was 1/9⅜d in Padiham in 1831; rent, fuel, candles, sizing etc. per head cost 6⅛d, so that the average amount left for food was 1/3¼d. In 1833 there were 1381 workers and 4 unemployed yet with the 1832 franchise Padiham had only 27 voters, i.e. those householders paying a rental of £10 per annum.

Fig. 25
Robert Shuttleworth

Fig. 26 Robert's wife Janet
and daughter Janet

Burnley Mill.

Whereas,

Divers Persons who owe Suit at the Ancient Mill called Burnley Mill, situate in the Township of *Burnley*, in the County Palatine of Lancaster, have lately neglected to do Suit at the said Mill, and have ground Wheat, Beans, Oats, Barley, or other Grain, or made Oats into Groats, or ground Groats into Meal, or made or ground Malt, or have carried their Grist to other Mills, contrary to the Rights, Privileges, and Prerogatives of the said Ancient Mill, and contrary to the Ancient Custom there. Now we the Undersigned, Attornies, as well of *Thomas Woodhead*, the present Miller and Farmer of the said Ancient Mill, as of *Janet Shuttleworth*, an Infant, and of the Trustee and Guardian of the said Infant, the Proprietors of the said Ancient Mill, Do hereby give you Notice, that Proceedings at Law will be taken against all Persons whomsoever owing Suit at the said Mill who shall henceforth neglect to perform the same according to the Ancient and Lawful Custom. And that a Copy of the Letters Patent of his late Majesty King *James the First*, under the Great Seal of England, the Seal of the County Palatine of Lancaster, and the Seal of the Duchy of Lancaster, bearing date at Westminster, the Eleventh Day of February, in the 7th Year of his said Majesty's Reign, is deposited with *Mr. James Whittaker*, the Agent of the Proprietors, at Gawthorpe Hall, within Habergham Eaves, in the said County, for the perusal and inspection of all Persons interested in the same. Dated the *Twelfth* Day of *March*, 1836.

To the Inhabitants of the
Townships of Burnley
and Habergham Eaves.

Fig. 28 1836 Burnley Corn Mill Notice

CHAPTER 8

THE HEIRESS OF GAWTHORPE

Robert's eldest son, James, received Barton Lodge on Robert's death in 1814 and his second son, also called Robert (Fig.25), received Gawthorpe and the other estates. This Robert was the chairman of Preston Quarter Sessions and was called 'The People's Magistrate'. He moved into Gawthorpe after the death of his father and brought back the family portraits, plate and library. He married Janet, daughter of Sir John Marjoribanks, in 1816. Young Janet (later to marry Dr. James Kay) was born in 1817 (Fig.26) but Robert died in 1818 and was buried in Padiham Church where there is a tablet to his memory. In 1825 his wife remarried, this time to Fredrick North Esq., and this gentleman's diary contains some interesting items. On Wednesday, May 25th 1824 he wrote, 'Janet writes me that she is anxious to keep up Gawthorpe for the child (young Janet) at least so as to make it an occasional residence. This is well, and little Janet's advantage, whom I really love not only for her mother's sake but absolutely for her own, will be promoted. Expense is not to be considered and I desire Janet to think so for it is absurd to think that Chancery will allow aught if the Will directs the house to be for Mrs. Shuttleworth's benefit or else to be left for the child.' On Wednesday, July 6th, he was at Gawthorpe and wrote 'I cannot wholly understand the strange feeling which being at this place excites in me. There is something very painful in it. And yet, like many other painful feelings which excite at all events they do not even irritate the mind. I cannot keep myself from indulging in it. I have felt them before once or twice. There is a picture in the library which I cannot doubt to be that of Robert Shuttleworth from his likeness to Janet (the child presumably) which disturbs my mind in the strangest manner. It is a weakness, and one that must be combatted to the harsh, rather powerful and very intelligent countenance but showing much ill-temper and by no means of the liberal cast. Janet to have been under the control of such a character and yet having been so for him to have said as he did say on his death bed *'Marry again soon, you must make any man happy, if that man can make himself'*. She is indeed of a noble character and I will endeavour to render myself worthy of her."

The Burnley corn mill was still causing problems for the Shuttleworths. As owners of the mill they were concerned that other inhabitants were infringing their rights. Compared with the position in the 1400's the rolls were now reversed!

In 1836 a notice was issued by Janet's Trustees and Guardians to the inhabitants of the townships of Burnley and Habergham Eaves regarding Burnley Mill (Fig.28). The ancient corn mill, which had been bought by Colonel Richard Shuttleworth in 1611 was still in the hands of the Shuttleworth family and the miller at that time was Thomas Woodhead. The notice complained that the inhabitants of Burnley and Habergham Eaves were neglecting to grind their grain at the Soke Mill and had 'Carried their grist to other mills, contrary to the rights and pre-rogatives of the said ancient mill.'

Actions were taken against a number of people for contravention of these rights. These included Robinson Greenwood and John Greenwood owners of two steam corn mills. The steam corn mills had been built in 1822 and 1825 and from 1808 to 1822 Robinson and John had been servants of the tenants of the Soke Mill, which had become steam driven in 1820.

Janet, the heiress (Fig.27), wrote the following poem on the Long Gallery in 1838, when she was twenty one.

THE LONG GALLERY, GAWTHORPE

Beloved old Home, I leave thee, to return
I know not when; with saddened step, I pace
This gallery, and gaze on either wall
With looks of sorrow and with feelings deep.
The pictures of my ancestors appear
To look upon me with an unusual air,
Each seems a well-known and a valued friend,
Each seems to speak with kindness and with love.

Oh Gawthorpe, mine own Home, where first I saw
The beauteous light of Heaven, where first I heard
The voice of human beings in mine ear,
A meaningless and yet a pleasant sound;
Where first mine infant tongue was taught its use-
Oh well-loved Gawthorpe, none but GOD who made
My heart to love thee, can e'er fathom half
The love I bear thee, May my GOD forgive
If I too much adore my earthly Home
And thus forget my hoped-for Home in Heaven.

Backcloth to Gawthorpe

Mayst thou be blest, dear Gawthorpe, blest to me
And all who live here, May my love for thee
Be made a blessing. May I live and die
Within these walls, my life be one of peace,
Of Christian peace, and holy usefulness;
And when the hour of death is come to me
May peace and joy be mine, and may my death
Be blest to me and those I leave behind;
Father of mercy, let my prayer be heard.

Farewell, my own dear Gawthorpe, for a time;
Oh, may I soon return, with mind improved,
With heart yet more impressed with holy Faith,
With fewer thoughts of earth and more of Heaven;
With powers of usefulness matured and firm.
May my religion pure and undefiled
Be found within my home, within, without
On all sides flourishing, May Christian faith
Abound, and may this little spot become
A very Paradise, a Heaven on Earth,
A blessed portion of GOD'S Soverignty.
JANET SHUTTTLEWORTH

(Unfortunately her life at Gawthorpe did not prove to be so idyllic, she spent the last fifteen years of her life living apart from her husband on the Continent where she died, aged fifty five, and is buried.)

Janet was concerned about the education of the children of the area, and in 1840, at the age of twenty three, erected important additions to Gawthorpe school, Habergham, on the edge of Gawthorpe estate. Her initials and the date can still be seen over the doorway. She had written to the Board of Education for advice in 1839 and corresponded with its first Secretary, Doctor James Philip Kay.

On 24th February 1842 she married James Phillips Kay (Fig.29) who assumed the name and arms of Shuttleworth in addition to those of Kay. James Kay-Shuttleworth had been a doctor in Manchester and had also founded the Battersea Training College for teachers before his marriage. Hewas the first Secretary of the Board of Education and continued his interest in education throughout his life. In 1846, together with James and John Dugdale they had All Saint's Church, Habergham, erected next to the school. Janet had a particular interest in both Habergham church and school.

Fig. 27 The Heiress of Gawthorpe   Fig. 29 Sir James Kay Shuttleworth

Fig. 30 The Entrance Hall Fireplace

In 1850 James was made a baronet. The Shuttleworths and Dugdales helped to finance the running of the school until 1898 when it was taken over by Burnley School Board. They also helped to build Partridge Hill School in Padiham.

In the late 1840's the young Lady Kay Shuttleworth, according to family tradition, used to visit a little china shop in Burnley whose owner had been in service with the Brontes at Haworth. It was there that she heard about the wonderful young ladies at the vicarage and when 'Jane Eyre' was published, Lady Kay Shuttleworth read it and was convinced that Charlotte Bronte had written it. Intrigued by this, Sir James and his wife drove across the moors to Haworth and met old Mr. Bronte in the church. They were introduced to Charlotte and invited up to the vicarage. On the way up he spoke to her of the book. He later told his family that she was highly insensed, for old William Bronte, and no one else, knew at the time. Sir James invited her to Gawthorpe but she was reluctant to accept. Her father thought that a change of scenery would be good for her - her two sisters and brother had died by this time - and it was on his suggestion that she finally visited Gawthorpe. In a letter written on returning on March, 22nd 1850 she stated that *'My visit to Gawthorpe has left me certain images, certain pictures pleasant to contemplate. Your gray stately Hall fills one page of my mental sketch book ----'*

and in another:-

'---- the dialogues by the old fireside in the antique oak-panelled drawing room, while they suited Sir James, did not too much oppress and exhaust me. The house, too, is much to my taste; nearly three centuries old, gray, stately and picturesque!'

It was in August of that year that Lady Kay Shuttleworth introduced Charlotte to Mrs. Gaskell. This was when the two novelists stayed with the Kay Shuttleworths at Briary Close, above Windermere.

Charlotte again stayed at Gawthorpe after her marriage to the Rev. Nicholls, the curate at Haworth. It was at this time, January 1855, that Sir James offered Mr. Nicholls a living at Habergham. Unfortunately, Mr. Nicholls felt that he could not leave old Mr. Bronte and shortly after her return Charlotte fell ill and died on 31st March 1855.

By 1850 the principal estates of the Shuttleworths in Padiham were Northwood, Northwood Head, Copthurst, High Whitaker, Stockbridge, Tinklers or Old Moss, Nearer Bendwoodgrove, Cross Bank Farm and Scholebank.

The end of Burnley Soke Mill came in 1852 when it burned down and cotton spinning and weaving sheds were built on the site, retaining the old name of Kings Mill.

Fig.31

Fig.32

Gawthorpe before the Barry Restoration of 1850

Fig. 33 The Minstrels Gallery

Fig. 34 The Wooden Tablet of 1604

CHAPTER 9

THE BARRY RESTORATION

Sir James commissioned Sir James Barry in 1850 to restore the Hall, which had been neglected during the long minority of his wife. Barry suggested that it needed a 'frame' (Figs.31 & 32) and erected the parapets. He also lifted the tower a storey to accommodate the maids, and had the mottoes of the two families - *'Kind friends know and keep'* and *'Prudence and Justice'* placed on it in stone.

When Barry restored the building he removed a small panelled bedchamber behind the Minstrels Gallery, in order to carry the entrance hall to the south eastern angle of the building. Over the fireplace of this bedroom was the tablet (Fig.34) inscribed :-

	Shuttleworth		Shuttleworth		
	Lawrence	Elizabeth 1443	Nicholas	Ellen 1473	
G	Shuttleworth		Sir Richard	Margery 1599	L
N E	Hugh	Anne 1577	Knight	Sepultus	T T
	Lawrence	Shuttleworth	Shuttleworth		
	Presbytor	1545 Natus	Thomas	Ann 1586	
	Richard Shuttleworth	Nicholas Shuttleworth	Ughtred Shuttleworth 1604		

The initials on each side are family connections with the Grimshaws of Clayton (Hugh's wife Anne was formerly Anne Grimshaw) and the Levers of Little Lever (Thomas's wife Anne was formerly Anne Lever who had a brother Thomas Lever. He married Thomasine Heath) The Grimshaws heir living in 1604 was called Nicholas who had married Elizabeth Rishworth.
(This panel is now in the front hall at Gawthorpe.)

Two panels opened through the wall separating this 'Wainscot' room from the Music Gallery (Fig.33) and the occupant could observe what was passing in the dining hall. Probably these openings were used at an early period by the Lady of the House to overlook her servants at work in the Hall, but in times of peril they would also enable any person to see whether the Hall was clear of dangerous guests, whilst from the window on the South and the small mullioned window on the East two sides of the Hall might be inspected. The sill of the mullioned window on the eastern side of this apartment had been opened and two large headed iron nails driven through the sill into the wall below. This had been done roughly and in haste. When workmen came to remove the sill they had to prize it open with some force and they found a heap of gold coins, chiefly Portuguese of John V reign bearing dates 1709-1745, but there were also coins of Peter II Portugal and Charles II; James II; William III; Anne; George I; and George II of England. There was no coin of a later date than 1745. We know that Col. Francis Towneley in 1745 preceded the descent of the Pretender's troops to Lancashire by a mission to the leading gentry of the County who had connections by blood with his family, or whose religion inclined to the House of Stuart. Col. Towneley may have been a guest at Gawthorpe and might have received a message necessitating a speedy departure. After meeting Bonnie Prince Charlie in Manchester, Towneley and his regiment set out for Derby but there he was given orders to retreat and was commissioned to defend the city of Carlisle. Subsequent to its surrender he was executed and his head was impaled upon Temple Bar in London. His fate would account for the coins remaining at Gawthorpe.

Another of Barry's features was the plaster ceiling with the Kay Shuttleworth initials in the Great Hall, together with the fireplace and incorporated shields (Fig.38):-

Shuttleworth arms	Kay	Barton arms (from Fleetwood)
Shuttleworth arms differenced	Shuttleworth	Kirk arms (from Jane)
Kay arms	Achievement	Clerke arms (from Catherine - the Infanta)
Kay Shuttleworth arms		Holden arms (from Mary of Aston Hall)

The fireplace with Sir James Kay Shuttleworth's children's initials incorporated, including the 1st Lord Shuttleworth's (Ughtred) in the centre, was placed in the then entrance hall at this time (Fig.30). The front door itself was heightened (Fig.35), a window put above it, and both Kay and Shuttleworth emblems can be seen there too. The library and staircase were also modernised.

A description of Gawthorpe in 1858 stated that the house was a lofty embattled pile, with large and bay windows of many lights. The Hall was covered with lead and surmounted by a single turret in the middle of the roof. The plasterwork with deep cornices and assorted stalagmites was rich and entire. The fireplaces were of the original massive stonework each with elevated hearths and stone ridges which rendered fenders unnecessary. On the fourth floor of the house looking south was the gallery 25 yards long in which were placed numerous family portraits. Amongst these was the founder in a clergyman's habit, with the Arms and differences of a second brother. Next was brother Thomas in a turnover collar exactly resembling that of the portraits of Shakepeare and his Lady, a Lever, in a large ruff. After this pair was a very handsome pair of portraits, namely Richard Shuttleworth, Esq., about 50 years old, in a plain puritan outfit, and his lady, heiress of Barton, in a high crowned hat, on the top of a very elaborate headdress. His son, Capt. William Shuttleworth, who was killed fighting for Parliament, appeared in armour with smoke and an indistinct view of the engagement in the background. After this were several of later date. In the dining room below was an excellent painting by Wright of Derby of James Shuttleworth, Esq., (great grandfather of the then owner), his lady and daughter.

The description goes on to say that before the alterations of the house by Barry the door was in the recess of a low porch within which was a stone seat on either side of it. It was of massive oak, the planks of which were held together by strong iron bolts with square heads for outer face. Two larger iron hinges stretched across it and it was bolted by a ponderous wooden bar which rested in holes cut in either jamb. This entrance lead through a passage to an oaken stair which wound upwards in the panelled interior of the tower to the several storeys. Soon after the beginning of the 19th century the staircase had fallen so much out of repair that it was removed altogether, together with the oaken panels. This part of the house was then replaced in a style inconsistent

Fig. 35 The Modified Entrance

Fig. 36 The Rich Stone Screen

with the rest of the structure. Sir Charles Barry restored the whole of the entrance to a strictly Elizabethan style, though more decorated than the original. The arch of the front porch was raised so as to afford space for mullion windows above, and the door was brought forward so as to enclose the ancient internal porch of the entrance hall. Over the entrance, in the frieze was the Kay motto in old English characters, and above this three square stone panels, The centre one was evidently the stone carved by the joiner mentioned in the accounts. It bore on the shield the three shuttles surmounted by the Shuttleworth crest, with helmet and mantling and over all was the date 1605. The dexter panel (on the right) bore the arms of Kay, the sinister panel those of Shuttleworth and Kay quarterly. Inside the Tudor arch doorway to correspond with the motto outside was that of the Shuttleworths - *Prudentia et Justicia*. The door lead to a stone vestibule decorated on the west side with a carved armourial shield, while on the east through an open oak screen there was a panelled entrance hall surrounded by family portraits. (The open oak screen was replaced with an enclosed panelled screen by the 4th Lord Shuttleworth when the entrance hall formerly on the east side of the vestibule was converted into a kitchen after the Second World War). The hallway leads through a rich stone screen (Fig.36), to a passage divided from the interior of the tower by a second screen of the same material. These were erected to hold the increased weight of the tower. On the right was the dining room, on the left was the drawing room and passing through the second screen into the interior of the tower you approached the library.

The 1858 description gives further details of the entrance hall, which was again altered after the Second World War.

'That part of the entrance hall screened off from the vestibule was a long room in the east wing with a deep semi-octagonal recess. Before Sir James Kay Shuttleworth commenced the renovation of the hall this apartment was divided into several small rooms and it is believed that it is now restored to its original dimensions, and further improved by opening a window above the fire-place. The apartment is oak panelled with a geometrical Tudor ceiling.

Above the panelling various family portraits covered the north wall. (In 1953 Lord Shuttleworth and his family removed to Leck Hall and took all the family portraits). The panelling was used partly to solidify the western end of the room dividing it from the actual entrance. Also on the north wall was a panel consisting of a series of initials (Fig.34).

Fig.37 The Drawing Room Fireplace

Fig. 38 The Shields about the Fireplace
in the Great Hall

From the entrance hall two doors gave admission to the dining hall which occupied the greater part of the east wing of the house on the principal floor having a larger semi-octagonal recess or oriel at its upper and looking east, and an open gallery over its lower end. Some windows which had been blocked up were opened and the room greatly improved. It retained its oak panelling but the handsome stone chimney piece was Barry's idea. The geometrical ceiling of the roof was restored and the pendants greatly enriched.

On the spandrills to two Tudor archways to the doorways to the room were four small heraldic shields commemorating Hugh and his three sons. (There was a fourth child Ellen or Eleanor who married a Nowell.)

The drawing room occupied the whole front of the west wing. It was surrounded by panels richly decorated and inlaid with wood lighter or darker than oak. The lower panels over the fireplace had the initials of the chief connections of the family (Fig.37) at the period when the house was built :-

WALMSLEY	HALSALL	SHUTTLEWORTH	SHUTTLEWORTH	OSBALDESTON
THOS. ANNE	THOS. JANE	RICH. M'GRET	ROBERT ANNE	ED. MATHILDA
			or RICHARD	Dau. of Sir
KNIGHT	KNIGHT	KNIGHT		Thomas HALSALL

Above the panelling which reaches to within 18 inches of the ceiling there was a deep plaster frieze grotesquely decorated which supported the ceiling covered in a rich vine pattern on which clusters of grapes grouped as pendants. At intervals in the plaster frieze were figures in the costumes of different ranks of the people of the reign of Elizabeth and at angles lions and gryphons held shields. Figures of Sir Richard and Margaret were over the fireplace (Figs.9 & 10).

On the first floor there were several chambers. On the wall of the principal room was a stone shield dated 1600 - 1603. All the rooms on this floor had ceilings in geometrical forms.

On the second floor the long gallery extended the whole length (70 feet x 30 feet) of the south front to which it had three oriels. There were seven latticed windows, mostly containing the original glass and quaint handles for opening the casement. (For window tax payments the stone mullions were counted, so this room paid tax on 94 windows.) The fireplace stood centrally, one panel containing the Royal arms with the letters J.R. 1603 (Fig.12). Two inscriptions below, one being :-

'Fear God, Honour the King, Eschew Evil and Do Good,
'Seek Peace and Ensue it.'

The Great Barn's dimensions, lofty roof and columnar supports gave to the interior the character of a spacious church with side aisles and oak timbered roof, unquestionably the largest and finest barn for many miles around and evidently contemporary with the Hall (Fig.14).

From the preceding full description of the Hall in 1858 we may note that the only major structural alterations carried out in the following hundred years were made by the 4th Lord Shuttleworth to the entrance after the Second World War.

During the cotton famine of 1861-5 Sir James Kay Shuttleworth was on the Cotton Famine Relief Committee and employed weavers on the grounds outside the Hall, the plans of which had been prepared by Barry but not put into effect. His philanthropic works included the provision of a drinking fountain to Burnley, placed at the bottom of Manchester Road by the 'Gawmless' gas standard and he also acted as mediator to settle the Padiham miners' strike of 1860. He was also the first President of the Burnley Literary and Philosophical Society founded at the Mechanics Institute in which he had a great interest and was life governor of the Burnley Grammar School. In 1863 he was made High Sheriff of Lancashire and wrote the novels 'Scarsdale' & 'Ribblesdale'.

Sir James and Janet had four sons and one daughter born between 1843 and 1851 and their initials are inscribed in the fire-place at Gawthorpe dated 1856 (Fig.30).

During the restoration of Gawthorpe the children had lived at their London residence, 38 Gloucester Square, with Janet and their governess Miss Poplawska. Janet never saw Gawthorpe fully restored as she lived mainly abroad from 1853 and never returned to her old home. She died and was buried in Germany in 1872.

Fig. 39 The Spiral Staircase

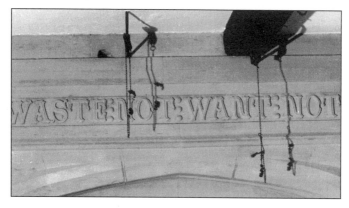

Fig. 40 The Kitchen Range in the Basement

CHAPTER 10

THE LATE VICTORIAN PERIOD

Ughtred (Fig.45), the eldest son of Sir James and Janet Kay Shuttleworth went into Parliament at 23 years of age and married Blanche Marion Parish (Fig.46) four years later, in 1871, in Hastings, for which borough he was M.P. On his return home with his bride he disembarked at Burnley Barracks station and the farmers and estate workers, on horseback with green cockades in the horses' ears (green being the livery colour of the Shuttleworths), lined the road from the Tim Bobbin Hotel at Ightenhill to the gates of Gawthorpe. The weavers in the area also appeared to have had a half-day holiday for this event though whether they were paid for this privilege is uncertain. There was a party for the tenants in the Great Barn at Gawthorpe and a silver candelabra was given to the bride and groom. In response to one of the toasts, one speaker said that he remembered the first cotton mill to be built in Padiham, with a 10 h.p. engine called "Bold Venture". The same speaker also took the opportunity to inform his landlord that the local streets were not generously paved and that the sewers needed improving!

Sir James had refurnished the boudoir at Gawthorpe for his daughter-in-law. All the new furniture was in white, painted with little flowers, quite a novelty in the days of heavy mahogany furniture.

James continued to reside at Gawthorpe until Janet's death the following year, 1872, two days before her first grand-child was born, Ughtred's eldest child Angela. The estates passed to Ughtred on Janet's death and Sir James went to the shooting box built on a beautiful site on their estates at Barbon near Kirkby Lonsdale where James resided until his death in 1877, aged 73.

Ughtred and Blanche had six children, four girls and two boys, born between 1872 and 1894. Their style of living at the end of the nineteenth century can be measured by the reminiscences of two of the girls, Angela and Rachel, and the writings of their friend Mrs. John Brown.

Fig. 41 The Entrance to the Estate Office

Fig. 42 The roof of the Estate Office

The following excerpts from the writings of Mrs. John Brown serve admirably to describe the Gawthorpe scene at the end of the nineteenth century.

One of the great delights of my life at that time was visiting Gawthorpe Hall, home of Sir Ughtred and Lady Kay-Shuttleworth. It was a centre of refreshment, refinement, and restoration for my husband and me for all the long years we lived in Lancashire. I saw Lady Kay-Shuttleworth for the first time soon after we came to Burnley and thought her the loveliest woman I had ever seen. It was at a Garden Party at Bankhall, she interested me there and then. Later on she talked to me about the old Burnley Workhouse Infirmary. She had heard it was a dark spot and that something was needed.

I shall take these soft shades of grey for the stone walls of this dear old hall with its turrett and mullion windows and these colours of crimson and yellow and dark green, for the virginia creepers and ivy grew about the walls and pillars near the great oak doorway. Over this doorway are letters in olde english, and there are in bas relief some weavers! shuttles, the crest of the Shuttleworth family. Charlotte Bronte visited the first Lady Kay-Shuttleworth at Gawthorpe, and it was Sir James and Lady Kay-Shuttleworth who first introduced her to Mrs. Gaskell, when they were fellow guests of theirs at The Briary, Ambleside. The friendship of the Shuttleworth family, who spent many months of the year at Gawthorpe Hall, was a beautiful feature of our life in Lancashire and extended over many years. Opportunities were given us to meet interesting and distinguished people, and there my philanthropy grew and received fresh impulse and stimulus. Gawthorpe and all it meant had made a delightful contrast in our lives. I returned from scenes in the workhouse or from a meeting of Co-operative Guilds to a dinner party at Gawthorpe where we heard much of the best books, of politics, of social questions and music, and had many interesting discussions. Looking back, I realise how refreshing it all was. I owed as much to the reality then as to the memory now, God gives us roses in Summer and we have memories in Winter. Looking back now, though it was 35 years ago, (this was written in 1921) the light and life of that old hall and its dear inmates still shed a radiance on us and on our days, though the forms and faces seem to cloud a bit that we met in those days, some that have been identified in literature, church and state. We met Judge Hughes there the author of Tom Brown's Schooldays, a book which he gave me, as nothing else did, a word picture of the great Dr. Arnold. I think one of the most fascinating men I met at Gawthorpe was Mr. Wm. Arnold, brother of Mrs. Humphrey Ward, he was one of the editors of the Manchester Guardian. The present Lord Shuttleworth was an ardent follower of Mr. Gladstone.

It was at Gawthorpe that I met Sir Edward, later Viscount Grey and his beautiful wife. It was arranged that I should meet them at lunch and then drive with her to see the workhouse and the mill. Lady Grey was like one of Burne-Jones' beautiful women with her long throat and lovely shaped head, with a knot of rich auburn hair low down on her neck. She was killed in all the charm and gladness of her youth by accident. I remember Sir Ughtred speaking to me of Sir Edward Grey and saying that Mr. Gladstone regards him as one of the promising young liberals. I owe one of the happiest events of my life to Lord and Lady Shuttleworth when I made my first visit to Italy with them, as their guest. (This is in the Winter 1891/2)

In 1883 Lady Shuttleworth and Mrs. John Brown took up the cause of young girls who were in moral danger and founded a 'House of Help' in Padiham Road, later in Todmorden Road and Bank Parade. This was continued in later years by the Honourable Rachel Kay-Shuttleworth. Lady Shuttleworth also formed a District Nursing Association in Padiham and Habergham, one of the earliest in England.

At this period the Gawthorpe household consisted of a Butler, 2 footmen, an 'oddman', a cook housekeeper (Fig.40), 2 kitchen maids, a scullery maid, two housemaids and a lady's maid for Lady Shuttleworth, plus one for the sisters. There was a head nurse and an under nurse in the Nursery and later a governess. On the estate there was an Estate Office, run by the Agent and an Assistant, a laundry run by a washerwoman and her two daughters, a gardener and four under gardeners with a boy apprentice, a coachman, and undergrooms and a carter.

The livery was green with silver buttons with the Coat of Arms in silver, but outdoors buff was used. The women servants and head housemaid slept in the tower, except for the lady's maid who slept within reach. The men slept in the basement, the butler in the pantry with the plate, and the rest in the servants' hall on folding beds. Two of the butlers over this period were called

Fig. 43 The Estate Cottages

Fig. 44 Memorial to Charles Camm

Wareham and Winkfield. The 'odd man' who was called Tommy Wickham at the turn of century was responsible for the odd jobs including making ice, cleaning boots, silver and lamps. There were 40 lamps at this time and Tommy had to start after breakfast and clean them all, filling them with colza oil for safety. In the evenings when they were lit it was the footmen's job to 'wind them up' every hour. These lamps continued to be used until the 1920's when electricity was installed. Coal fires had also to be placed in the ground floor rooms and parent's nursery, head housemaid, housekeeper and lady's maids rooms, although all rooms could not be so heated and the girls had to learn to 'dress quick'. A form of central heating had been used since the 1850's. The first was a large cylindrical drum placed in the well of the stairs and lit by heated coke, but this filled the house with smoke. The next was a boiler in the basement, which heated air-vents up the tower and all the way to the linen room, but this broke down in the 1920's. For the wings of the house there was no separate system until the 1960's when electric storage heaters were installed.

The servants had their own hierarchy. One never gave orders to anyone but the head servants, which was at times most inconvenient. There were certain privileges. All had meals in the servants' hall, for example, but the housekeeper retired 'grandly' to the housekeeper's room for her pudding! The scullery maids also had their 'perks'. They were allowed to keep the rabbit skins when they skinned a rabbit and these were sold to the pedlars. This, of course, augmented their wages. The servants were paid once a quarter, the younger maids getting their age in pounds once a year. At Christmas their gift would be a Prayer book or Bible, and a roll of material for their next Sunday dress. The Cook Housekeeper had to be able to order food as well as cook it, and she ordered from London where the quality was better in those days than it was locally. All jobs were meticulously apportioned. The first and second footmen's work was settled by the butler. The second footman carried up meals to the nursery on the second floor where the nanny was to be found with her young charges. One nanny, namely Mrs. Matthews, was notorious for being terribly afraid of thunder and lightning, and she used to huddle all the children into the linen cupboard with her during storms, and tell them stories to way-lay their fears, which were much less than hers! The children thoroughly enjoyed these ventures. The nursemaid, however, was not allowed in the cupboard until she had hidden the knives.

The nursemaids tasks included carrying up endless cans of hot water from the basement to the second floor for the hip-baths, and then carrying down the cold water again. As a further penance this had to be done by the spiral staircase (Fig.39), which the servants disliked because it made them dizzy. The hip baths were stored in the 'bathroom' by the day nursery. It was the housemaids job to carry up the water for the ladies of the household and this task continued until 1900 when a bath was installed on the first floor. Thereafter both the family and servants could bathe there, the servants having to use the bathroom when the family were out; and to leave it immaculate. In later years a second bathroom was installed by the Butler's bedroom in the basement for the use of the servants.

The footmen also travelled on the carriage, escorted the younger members of the family and knocked on the door on arrival at the destination. If a footman became engaged to a maid of the same house, the protocol was for one to leave the household. The maids, of course, had their work designated by the housekeeper. They had to be good packers and travellers and the lady's maid was usually French or Swiss, and acted as a Courier when the family travelled abroad.

All the servants were required to go to Church every Sunday, and to attend family prayers each morning at which time they came into the room in strict precedence.

In the evening the maids and the daughters of the family would gather in the drawing room into which a fire had been put by the footmen, and they would sit around the large table with the lamp in the middle. They sewed red flannel petticoats for the poor, these were cut out by the lady's maid. One of the daughters, or the lady of the house, read chapters from a 'good book' and then after that from something jolly like "Three men in a Boat". The head housemaid also had a lamp to do the mending, and the underhousemaid had to help her.

In the Elizabethan cottages (Fig.43) by the back tunnel entrance to Gawthorpe lived the coachman, under-gardeners, the carter and the laundry family. The coachmen at this period were very popular with Ughtred's children . In the 1870's the coachman was a man named Shepherd, When his daughter was born, he asked Angela, the eldest daughter of Ughtred, still only a young child herself, to name the baby. She named her Ailsie. His wife died shortly afterwards and Ailsie was later brought into the nursery as a young nurse-maid. After Shepherd came Charles Camm, a great favourite with the children, who used to visit his cottage. In those days the coachman's cottage had a tiny wooden staircase, and one daughter lived upstairs. It had two bedrooms, flagged floors and an old range. There were rag rugs on the floor, a scrubbed table, plain kitchen chairs and two rockers. The Camms' travelled with the Shuttleworths, they had a cottage at Barbon, and were housed in the mews in London. Mrs.Camm sometimes acted as chaperone to the girls at dances and up to Church. Camm reputedly had a way with horses, and would deal with the ailments of humans in the same way! (He always said that he would serve Lady Shuttleworth as long as she lived and, in fact, died in the same month as she did in August 1924. Lord Shuttleworth had a plaque to Camm's memory erected in Habergham Church (Fig.44), for he had served Gawthorpe for 34 years; a plaque to Lady Shuttleworth was erected by the parishoners in Habergham Church.)

At right angles to the coachman's cottage, separated by the old stables, unused since the 1850's when the barn stables were used and a new coach-house built, was the laundry at Gawthorpe. Here, up to the turn of the century, resided the laundry family; they were responsible for the estate laundry, whether the Shuttleworths were in residence at Gawthorpe, London or Barbon. Laundry travelled from London or Barbon in huge baskets by train each week, the carter bringing it from the station. This method was cheaper than having separate laundry maids in London and Barbon.

In this court-yard too, lived the under-gardeners, the gardener having his own cottage by the greenhouses. McMaster (Fig.51) was a gardener of repute. He grew grapes in the vinery and orchids, pineapples, tomatoes and bananas which were a rare luxury in those days. These were grown in hot-houses which needed stoking throughout the night. The gardens were delightful to view for McMasters specialised in Chrysanthemums, indeed one reporter in 1888 quoted them as "an intricate mass of fantastic beds" (Fig.52); he still found time to look after the turtle doves, rabbits, pigeons and dogs, which were the children's pets and which were kept at the gardener's house. The under-gardeners had to be taught their craft, which included tree husbandry, vegetable growing, rose tending, and such meticulous tasks as laying out the many paths with sifted golden sand which the carter had to bring up from the river. This was raked regularly to give a suitable "frame" for the flower beds. Little wonder that McMaster was promoted to be head of Parks at Skelmersdale!

Above the under gardener's cottage was the Estate Office (Figs.41 & 42), where all the business for the Shuttleworth estates was transacted. The agents of those days had many and varied tasks, beside the upkeep of the halls and supervision of the grounds, they had to be adept at the various skills of forestry and mining, together with the supervision of roads and houses built over a large area of Padiham and areas around Ightenhill, Wheatley Lane and Fence. Farming varied on the various estates, and the Agent, Mr.Ford at this period, had to deal with dairy farming at Gawthorpe, sheep at Barbon, and cheese, eggs and pigs at Inskip in the Fylde.

On rent days the tenants, numbering about 70, were invited to dinner in the long gallery (Fig.47), where the children usually played with their old battered rocking horse became a dining room for 100 people, seated at tables on long benches. Sir Ughtred and the family sat at one end, the estate office staff at the other. There was goose or beef, plum pudding or apple pasties, cheese and celery with beer or ginger beer for the farmers. The toasts were drunk in cheap port so as not to encourage a taste for wine! (One key that was kept by the Master of the house and no one else was that of the Wine Cellar.) This was kept in a suitable cask in the basement especially for this occasion. The problem was how to serve the food piping hot from the basement three floors down. This was done by conscripting all the estate men, undergrooms, undergardeners, carpenter, labourers etc., and placing them on every third or fourth step up the spiral staircase (Fig.39) which turned five times and contained 80 steps! They passed up all the food, hand to hand, and the empty plates back down again. The speeches to the Farmers meanwhile, would include news of the family and the estates by Lord Shuttleworth, and a response by the senior tenant on the Estate, who would propose a toast to the family.

The dinners given to the guests of the Shuttleworths were usually smaller and were held in the Great Hall with the hosts and any special guests on the dias. Some of the more famous personages who were accorded this hospitality were Mr.Speaker Peel; Lord Grantham, The Chancellor of the Exchequer; H.C.E.Childers, John Bright, and the American Ambassador of the time. In 1913, King George V and Queen Mary had their luncheon there on their visit to Burnley, when Lord Shuttleworth was Lord Lieutenant of Lancashire. At a large dinner party there would be two alternative soups, fish, entree, meat or bird, sweet, savoury, etc. A great problem here was washing up. The plates could be stacked but the tiny copper saucepans brought from Paris, which held one mouthful of cheese souffle had both to be made individually and washed individually. The maid was responsible for these, the scullery maid and footmen each had to wash up certain things, and if the best dessert plates (the Chelsea, or old Chinese) were used, then the lady's maid personally descended to a special sink because these were very valuable. The children of the family were not allowed to attend these meals, but often, in their nightdresses, they would escape from the nursery and climb down the spiral staircase to the Minstrels Gallery (Fig.33). They would then creep in and lie on their stomachs watching and listening to the speeches until their Mother noticed them, when she would make a sign to the footmen who would chase them back to bed up the back stairs!

Fig. 45 The First Lord Shuttleworth

Fig. 46 Blanche Marion
Ughtred's wife

CHAPTER 11

THE FIRST LORD SHUTTLEWORTH

Sir Ughtred Kay Shuttleworth's philanthropic and educational interests were like his father's; he too provided a drinking fountain, this one to Padiham in 1888 placed at the corner of Victoria Road and Burnley Road. He also presented the Kay Shuttleworth collection of fossils to the Owens College, Manchester in 1894, these having their origins in local mine workings. He founded the Cancer Research Clinic at the Victoria Hospital in Burnley, was President of the Burnley Mechanics Institute, gave scholarships to the Burnley Grammar School, and the Padiham Technical School was built through his generosity. A grant of land from the eastern side of Gawthorpe estate enabled Ightenhill Park to be built and another grant from the southern side allowed for the tramway from Cheapside to Padiham to be built along Padiham and Burnley road.

During his political life he was Under Secretary of State for India and Parliamentary Secretary to the Admiralty. He was also Chairman of the Canals and Waterways Commission and in 1902 was created a baron and elevated to the House of Lords. In this atmosphere the children grew up, steeped in politics, and were well informed on all the current local questions; together with this, in the schoolroom, they had as part of their exercises to write copies of the letters sent by their father, as he always wrote in longhand, considering it ill-mannered to reply to a personal letter by typewriter.

Christmas was the time when the children of the gentry would be invited to Gawthorpe and have their party in the Great Hall. The children of the coachmen and gardeners were allowed to watch from the Minstrels Gallery and doubtless had their own party downstairs later.

Parties were such a treat in those days that they were usually followed by an epidemic, for parents would send their children well or unwell. On one occasion a party was said to be ruined by a large "whoop" from one of the neighbour's children; whooping cough was serious in those days. There were handbell ringers from Burnley on these occasions and the Glee Singers from Habergham used to sing in the gardens during this season. Sir Ughtred had

Backcloth to Gawthorpe

Fig. 47

Fig. 48
Gawthorpe at the End of the Nineteenth Century

seen Christmas trees when visiting his mother in Germany and each Year had one erected at Gawthorpe. These were reputedly the first in the North of England, although the Prince Consort had introduced them into Buckingham Palace some years earlier. They were loaned out afterwards to hospitals and churches, in strict rotation, and this was continued until 1939. There would be the presents and an apple and orange for each child, fruit being a luxury in those days.

Father would personally put every candle on the tree himself, some four hundred, individually wired, and whilst they were alight footmen stood around with long poles on which were placed wet sponges to dampen any fire that might result.

The family were always fire conscious. Blanche Kay Shuttleworth had her dress burned when a child and had a horror of fire. The household thus had regular fire drills, davits were attached to the upper tower windows for the maids who had to practice how to escape from the top of the tower by chute. One regular casualty of these practices were the maid's best black silk stockings which they insisted on wearing when the handsome men of the Fire Brigade came for practices; the stockings were invariably torn by the ropes on the descent! There was also a large bell on the East side of Gawthorpe up to the end of the first World War, when it came down and was taken out of use. It was rung in case of fire so that the farmworkers could help to quell the outbreak. This was not its only function, as it was also rung at certain hours of each day to inform the farmworkers and people around of the time.

Although the servants worked long hours life wasn't all work for them. In the Summer there were cricket matches on the cricket field in the "ings" which was the ground between the Hall and the river (before the river was moved back in 1959). The estate men, servants, Lord Shuttleworth and his sons played matches against local teams and in the evening, after the match there was a meal in the coach house, the food being cooked in the house and brought out through the tunnel, past the ice house where the game was kept cool. Later there would be a dance with a fiddler, the maids in their dark dresses of black or navy blue, trimmed with lace and the ladies making an appearance in their evening dresses and shawls. (They dressed, of course, every night for dinner.) The men would be wearing heavy shoes and the dances would necessarily consist of barn dances with an occasional polka. In winter, feasts were held in the servants' hall around Christmas, and then they came upstairs to the dining

Fig. 49 The Lovers' Seat on the Roof

Fig. 50 The Chaperone's Seat

room where a drugget would be put over the dining room carpet on which one could dance and even waltz.

The young ladies and gentlemen of the area had their Balls too, on the drugget, and their other pastimes at Gawthorpe included riding especially over the "ings" and through the woods beyond. There was shooting up to the 1900's when they gave up keepering the estate in favour of Barbon.

They attended social functions and interested themselves in social welfare work such as the "House of Help" and Infant Welfare. The girls usually were adept at some form of needlework, for example embroidery, and the young men attached themselves to the estate office for first hand knowledge of the estate management, which at Gawthorpe included going down mines and over the farms. When the local farms ware inspected the father and sons went around the shippons and outhouses and the mother and daughters inspected the cottages. When the young ladies were betrothed they were allowed to use the "lover's seat" on the roof (Fig.49), providing, of course, that the chaperone was behind on her own special seat! (Fig.50) Though the roof had its advantages in this respect, it had its disadvantages in Winter when the capilliary action of the moisture in the snow used to necessitate a gang of men clearing the snow from the lead joints on the roof, a none too pleasant task in the depths of winter - perhaps even in the dark!

Although Christmas was usually spent at Gawthorpe, on occasions it was spent at Barbon. August and September were also spent at Barbon for this was the shooting season. Gamekeepers taught the boys to shoot at both Inskip and Barbon. At Inskip, duck, snipe, pheasant, water hens, partridges and hares were shot; grouse was shot at Barbon.

When Parliament was sitting the family stayed in London at their house in Princes Gardens, South Kensington, now pulled down for University extensions. At Whitsuntide they were usually abroad, visiting such places as Paris, Turin, Rome, Naples and Pisa. The foreign travelling arrangements were usually left in the hands of a travel agency such as Cooks. Lady Shuttleworth never bought a railway ticket in her life, nor for that matter did she ever do her own hair.

For travel to Barbon or London where the whole household was involved, the arrangements were more complicated. Railways preferred to remove a large household all in one train, so a special train was ordered. They travelled either

Fig. 51 James McMaster

Fig. 52 The Gardens at Gawthorpe

on the N.W. railway or Midland route via Todmorden. All the family and the indoor servants went, as well as the coachman, the groom and the pony boy with a pair of carriage horses, two or three riding horses and a pony, various carriages, Mother's Victoria and a small landeau. Everything was packed and taken, apart from large furniture. Each member of the family had a large wooden box roughly a yard and a half by a yard by a yard; there was one also for the nurses and one for the school books. There were also five plate chests with padlocks and keys, each bound with iron and lined with green felt. These had special compartments for jugs, teapots, plates, knives and forks etc., and it was the butler's job to fill these. A careful check list was kept of all the items to prevent loss or pilfering. The children's baths were fitted with lids so that things could be packed in them; the children had a special box; the maids each had a tin trunk and the coach-man had one or more boxes. The Station brougham stayed a Gawthorpe; there was another brougham in London and a waggonette at Barbon. Before leaving, the lady of the house went around with the Estate Agent and he noted what she required to be done whilst the family was away, which rooms should be decorated, which carpets or curtains should be cleaned and any other details.

On the train, all the maids went in one or two carriages with a separate carriage for the children, governess and nanny and another for the parents and the secretary. The coachman, his wife and family were in yet another carriage. On the journey there were picnic lunches with cold chicken and cold rice pudding croquettes with jam inside. The children played games and "patience" or read whilst on the journey.

The caretakers were left in charge of Gawthorpe, usually a mother and daughter under the general supervision of the Estate Agent. They covered all the chairs each with its own canvas cover to protect the fabric. Everything else was covered or put in bags and fires were put in the rooms when required. From the gardens and hothouses at Gawthorpe, flowers and fruit were sent by rail to London or Barbon twice a week, Shortly after the First World War, the journeys by train stopped when the servant position changed.

Fig. 53 The First, Second and Third Lord Shuttleworths

Fig. 54 The Hon. Rachel Entertaining Visitors

CHAPTER 12

THE END OF AN ERA

The two sons of Lord Shuttleworth, Lawrence and Edward, had both been killed in 1917. Of the four daughters, three were now married and only Rachel was left at Gawthorpe with her Mother and Father. Lawrence had two sons, Richard and Ronald, and Edward had one son, Charles. The old traditions were still carried on as far as possible. St Matthew's school children still received a Bible from the family when they were leaving school, and mugs were given on special occasions. The Kay Shuttleworths were still concerned with social welfare in Padiham, and Rachel, together with such notables as "Major" Hargreaves and Father Hart, was busy with social work in the town; she was also County Commissioner for the Guides, and many rallies were held in the grounds of the Hall. She was not interested in horse riding and, with Camm the coachman becoming very old, her first car was bought about 1920. In 1922 came the Rolls Royce and the chauffeur, Longland, who drove it. Rachel was emerging as a needlewoman of note and her collection of craft work was increasing. Her interest in design was said to have been inspired by the ceilings at Gawthorpe, all of different designs, and the fact that as a child she had to sleep in various bedrooms, each with a differently designed ceiling; she was always moved out of her own bedroom when visitors came!

Lord Shuttleworth lived at Barbon in his old age. He was bedridden and blind and died aged 95 in 1939. Richard, Lawrence's son, then aged 24 became the second Baron Shuttleworth (Fig.53), but was killed in the Battle of Britain the following year, and his younger brother, Ronald, succeeded. He too was killed in action in 1942. Their cousin Charles (Fig.55) became the fourth Lord Shuttleworth, but was badly injured in the Western Desert, losing a leg and having the other paralysed. When he was finally invalided out he returned to a Gawthorpe being managed by Rachel in his absence, a Gawthorpe with few retainers. Structurally the house was totally unsuitable for a post war labour saving family. One great disadvantage was that the kitchen was situated in the basement, down the spiral staircase. Charles had the entrance hall (Fig.48) converted into a kitchen which he sealed off from the hall, using the woodwork from the entrance hall as a screen, including in it the initialled tablet originally above the fireplace in the small bedroom behind the minstrels gallery, which

Fig. 55 The Fourth Lord Shuttleworth

Fig. 56 Ann, Charles Ughtred's wife

Barry had removed in 1850 to give height to the entrance hall. He married Anne Phillips (Fig.56) and his heir, Charles Geoffrey was born in 1948.

When open cast mining commenced in the area around the Hall, Lord Shuttleworth decided to move and in 1952 bought Leck Hall, near Kirkby Lonsdale, his Mother being installed at Barbon Manor nearby. Rachel, who had moved to Fence, returned with her collection to Gawthorpe in 1954, making a flat for herself on the first floor with her Mother's boudoir as a lounge (Fig.54) and the house-keeper's room converted into a kitchen. Through the Gawthorpe Foundation she started to raise money to establish a residential craft centre at the Hall. Lord Shuttleworth offered gifts of the Hall and outbuildings and 7 acres of garden and woodland to the National Trust and Lancashire County Council to this end, and Rachel bequeathed her large collection of books, embroidery, lace, textiles and other crafts. Rachel died in 1967 and her dream was realised in 1970.

This indeed is a house with an historic future.

INDEX - PEOPLE

N.B. Names may appear more than once on a page

Marjoribanks	Janet	49
	John	49
Marshall		26
Matthews	Mrs.	71
Mikelbroke	William of	17
Monteagles	Lord	32
Morley	Lord	32
Nichols	Rev.	53
North	Frederick	49
Nowell		24, 63
Nutter	Christopher	29, 30
Osbaldeston	Edward	63
	Lawrence	40
	Matilda	63
Parish	Blanche	66
Parker		24, 30, 37
	Christopher	20
	Ellen	20
	G.	45
	John	18, 19
	Thomas	31
Paslew		30
	Francis	30
Pearson	Margaret	28
Peel	Mr. Speaker	74
Petre	Lord	30
Phillips	Anne	87
Pickup		20
Pollard	James	36
Prince Consort (Albert)		79
Queen Elizabeth 1		24, 32, 63
Mary		74
Radcliffe	Richard	40
Redfearn	Anne	29, 30
Richard	son of Matthew	17
Riley		28
Rishworth	Ellen	57
Robinson		26

Robinson	Edmund	30
Roe	John	36
Royle		24
Sager	John	45
Sankey	Widow	27
Sherburne	Edward	29
Shepherd		73
	Ailsie	73
Shuttleworth	Angela (Kay S)	66, 72
	Ann	30, 40, 57, 63
	Barton	40
	Bishop	30
	Blanche	66, 68, 69, 73, 79, 81, 85
(4th Lord)	Charles	61, 64, 85, 87
(5th Lord)	Charles G.	87
	Edward	37, 40
	Edward (Kay S)	85
	Elizabeth	41, 57
	Ellen	57
	Ellinor	40, 63
	Fleetwood	40, 41, 58
	Henry de	18
	Henry	31
	Hugh	20, 24, 25, 30, 57, 63
	James	43, 45, 49, 59
	Sir James Kay	51, 53, 59, 64, 66, 68
	Janet (Kay S)	49, 50, 51, 53, 64, 66, 68, 69
	Janet	49
	John	18, 37, 40
	Lawrence	20, 24, 25, 26, 32, 57
	Lawrence (Kay S)	85
	Margaret/Margery	40, 41, 57, 63
	Nicholas	20, 31, 37, 38, 40, 41, 57
	Rachel (Kay S)	66, 69, 85, 87
	Richard	41
	Richard of Hacking	30
	(Sir) Richard 1,	20, 24, 25, 26, 29, 30, 57, 63
	(Colonel) Richard	24, 29, 30, 31, 32, 35, 36 37, 38, 40, 50, 57, 59
	(Colonel) Richard (Jnr.)	37, 40
	Richard of Forcett	40
	(Sir)Richard 11	40, 41, 43, 45
	Richard (Ready Money)	43

Whittaker	Thomas	45
Whickham	Tommy	71
Wilkinson	Anthony	29
Willasell		26
	Ingram	26
Winkfield		71
Wood	Richard of the	17
	Roger	31
Woodhead	Thomas	50
Woodruffe	John	31
Worsley	Elizabeth	20
	Richard	20
Wright	of Derby	59
Yate	James	31
	Mr.	31
	Thomas	29, 31
Yates	Thomas	31

INDEX - PLACES